THE
SOVEREIGN
GOD
THAT ANSWER'S
BY FIRE.

THE GOD OF ELIJAH.

PASTOR NNAEMEKA C. UCHEGBU

THE SOVEREIGN GOD THAT ANSWER'S BY FIRE.
THE GOD OF ELIJAH.

iUniverse books may be ordered through booksellers or by contacting:

iUniverse
1663 Liberty Drive
Bloomington, IN 47403
www.iuniverse.com
844-349-9409

ISBN: 978-1-6632-5194-7 (sc)
ISBN: 978-1-6632-5195-4 (e)

Library of Congress Control Number: 2023905680

Print information available on the last page.

iUniverse rev. date: 05/15/2023

CONTENTS

ACKNOWLEDGEMENT

I wish to acknowledge my good friends Pastor William Maurice Johnson and his dear wife Donna Churcher, both of whom have been very wonderful sources of support to my spiritual journey. Their Sunday School Ministry (where they use my books as discipleship tools) wonderfully inspired me to sharpen my literary skills and encouraged my writing career. May God bless them abundantly.

INTRODUCTION

The word fire appears more than five hundred times in the complete version of the holy Bible. The repetitive mention of this versatile element therefore puts an incredible spotlight on its inevitable relevance to the natural man in the physical sphere, and its spiritual role as a key player in sacred religious worship.

In the Bible setting, the word fire generally refers to the manifestation of God's nature and actions in addition to other figurative forms such as light. But in secular parlance, fire represents a breathing flame with the various combustive characteristics that make it useful in most natural settings.

Fire is one of the most important elements in the world. This is because of its unique contributions to the domestic and the industrial arenas, and its role in sacred spiritual worship, where it occupies center stage as the major prevalent means for effective sacrificial worship.

From the spiritual perspective, fire is universally perceived as a symbol of power in most religions of the world. In the Christian religion and in Judaism, for instance, fire specifically represents Divine presence, Sovereign Majesty, Power, and the Glory of God (Exodus 3:2-3)

In the Old Testament tabernacle, the constant light produced from the golden lamp (the Menorah) was so synonymous with the presence of God that priests were specially assigned to ensure that the fire in the lamp burned without ceasing. Its light was a symbol of the ever-present glory of God.

But there are also several scriptures which describe other figurative functions of fire in the Bible. These symbolic forms of fire have often been used to connect God to actions such as baptism, cleansing and in other cases, his judgement. Thus, the Bible eloquently speaks of "baptism of fire" and "God's wrath of fire".

> *"John answered, saying unto them all, I indeed baptize you with water; but one mightier than I cometh, the latchet of whose shoes I am not worthy to unloose: he shall baptize you with the Holy Ghost and with fire:" (Luke 3: 16).*

> *"Circumcise yourselves to the LORD, and take away the foreskins of your heart, ye men of Judah and inhabitants of Jerusalem: lest my fury come forth like fire, and burn that none can quench it, because of the evil of your doings" (Jeremiah 4: 4).*

In heathen societies, where religious practices and cultural beliefs are built around seasonal festivals and ritual activities, fire is the prominent sacred tool of worship. In those pagan religions, fire is believed to represent the power and the wisdom of the gods.

Generally, the unique characteristics of fire remain the same. So, whether it is in the natural sphere where it serves human needs, or as an instrument of warfare in the spiritual realm, all fires possess the common abilities to bring sweet comfort or to cause horrible damage.

God is a holy and righteous being who hates sin with perfect hatred. He does not tolerate sin and would not endorse any form of iniquity among his children. So, those who survive constantly in his presence are people whose transgressions have been purged with his fire.

This fire cleanses the soul of believers from their carnal desires and other fleshly impurities that defile their bodies and make the walk with God dreary. The destruction of these evil yokes removes all things that make spiritual fellowship impracticable and render believers unusable by God.

CHAPTER 1

THE LIVING FIRE

Fire is one of the four major elements of nature. Others include water, dust, and air. There are more elements in nature, but without these four major ones, life would be drab, unexciting, and meaningless. So, these major elements hold the key to life. They add value to many areas of life in ways that make it worth the living.

Generally, natural fire is kindled when rapidly oxidized air encounters any combustive matter, such as wood, dry grass, gaseous substance, or oil. So, to start a natural fire, oxygen is necessary, in addition to the presence of a heat-generating source and some combustible materials.

Fire can be started intentionally or by accident. This means that it can be kindled by conscious human action, unconscious error, or by the spontaneous act of lightning. In some cases, fires have been linked with the mischievous acts of arsonists, by the programmed activities of sorcerers, or called down by prophets.

> *"While he was still talking, another messenger arrived and said, "Bolts of lightning struck the sheep and the shepherds and fried them—burned them to a crisp. I'm the only one to get out alive and tell you what happened." (Job 1: 16 MSG).*

From past centuries, fire has immensely contributed to human survival on earth. Early humans used stone to generate friction in the presence of naturally occurring air. This way, they lit fine tinder or saw dust. This was man's earliest way of making fire for cooking, hunting, or for heating their homesteads.

By rubbing flintstones together, humans created enough sparks and were able to start their fires. They did not have to worry about oxygen because the air in that epoch was highly oxidized. And they sustained the fire that was generated by supplying more air to the flame with makeshift fans.

Fire has supernatural power. And whether it is present in the spiritual or its physical state, in the good or bad form, it expresses itself in ways that cannot be ignored. However, it is good to know that in which ever form it manifests, all fires are under God's control.

Fire is a powerful tool that needs control even in its most ordinary form. Its roles in spiritual and physical forms illustrate the great influence it has on man and his environment. So, whether in its sacred use for ritual purposes, for traditional agriculture, or for land clearing, fire is a survival tool you cannot disregard.

Fire can literally hear, run, talk, and take instructions. Evidence of this is found mostly in spiritual warfare where it speaks the language of destruction. Once the spiritual fire is invoked (after prayers or relevant incantations), it will show up in the natural sphere as flames and perform its mission.

Even in the natural sphere, the use of hot water, hot air, hot metal plates or heated oil for the resolution of domestic disputes is highly discouraged. Many lives have been lost and marriages destroyed beyond repair, because someone failed to control their anger. Even the scripture compares God's anger to burning fire.

Some physical fires worthy of mention in this chapter include:

A). Wildfires.

In the year 2020, more than 4 million acres of land, excluding property and lives, was destroyed in the wake of a raging wildfire in the state of California. It is possible that the fire may have started by the spontaneous kindling of dry plants and trees due to lightning, as is sometimes the case in that area.

In the same year in Colorado, an abnormal wildfire almost ruined the entire city of "Ashland". In recent years, deaths from smog due to wildfires have become issues of highest concern. Many people suffer from asthma and other breathing problems, and the smoke released from these fires can lead to health complications.

Even with the best scientific developments, wildfire disasters have been difficult to predict, prevent, or fully control. And such fires have often led to terrible damage of incalculable proportions causing liver and kidney damage to those exposed to extended contact, in environments where they occur.

Another form of wildfire is the atmospheric "ghost light", generally known in folklore as "willow the wisp". This is a flame-like phosphorescence usually seen at night over swamps and mashes. Science explains that this is the product of gaseous escape due to the breakdown of organic matter buried beneath the soil.

But ancient folklore holds a different opinion as "willow the wisp" was believed to be the appearance of spirits. These scary spirits appeared mostly at dusk, dressed in dull, spiraling smoke. They are connected to wicked acts and are said to mislead late-night travelers who journey through forest areas.

In societies that practice ancestral worship, soul worship (which is animism), spiritism, and where they ascribe to the concept of reincarnation, there is the belief that the dead can appear among the living, for several reasons, to interact and communicate with their people.

The adherents of these religions believe in the "willow" phenomenon and venerate its appearance even though it is considered an evil omen. The sighting of the "willow" is often reported by people who journey through cemeteries, lonely farm pathways, or along the way to the stream.

Central to the claim by those who practice these religions is the idea that the spirit of the dead can be invoked to obtain information or to settle scores. They also believe that when the dead are not given proper funeral rights, their souls continue to roam about the earth sphere until their spirits are assuaged.

> *"And when Saul enquired of the LORD, the LORD answered him not, neither by dreams, nor by Urim, nor by prophets. Then said Saul unto his servants, Seek me a woman that hath a familiar spirit, that I may go to her, and enquire of her. And his servants said to him, Behold, there is a woman that hath a familiar spirit at Endor. And Saul disguised himself, and put on other raiment, and he went, and two men with him, and they came to the woman by night: and he said, I pray thee, divine unto me by the familiar spirit, and bring me him up, whom I shall name unto thee. And the woman said unto him, Behold, thou knowest what Saul hath done, how he hath cut off those that have familiar spirits, and the wizards, out of the land: wherefore then layest thou a snare for my life, to cause me to die? And Saul sware to her by the LORD, saying, As the LORD liveth, there shall no punishment happen to thee for this thing. Then said the woman, Whom shall I bring up unto thee? And he said, Bring me up Samuel. And when the woman saw Samuel, she cried with a loud voice: and the woman spake*

to Saul, saying, Why hast thou deceived me? for thou art Saul. And the king said unto her, Be not afraid: for what sawest thou? And the woman said unto Saul, I saw gods ascending out of the earth. And he said unto her, What form is he of? And she said, An old man cometh up; and he is covered with a mantle. And Saul perceived that it was Samuel, and he stooped with his face to the ground, and bowed himself." (1 Samuel 28: 6-14)

The Christian religion believes that physical death marks the end of life on earth. But the tenet of the Christian religion also holds that there is hope, on the resurrection morning, that a person will reconnect with their loved ones who lived and died in Christ.

Sadly, sorcerers and witches, like the witch of Endor, have for a long time dabbled into the eerie practice of invoking the spirits of the dead for pernicious reasons. Many who patronize them, believe these arts to be true. This has kept the concept of the "willow the wisp" alive as a spiritual phenomenon.

However, wildfires are regular occurrences in many parts of the world. In such places, scientists explain that they are due to natural, annual cycles caused by climate change. But in animist cultures, they believe it is a response by evil spirits who feel their privacy has been encroached.

B). Chemical fires.

Chemical fires, except in situations of military warfare, are unpredictable. And barring any human errors, this type of fire is preventable where there are adequate preparations. With better care, right personnel, and anti-fire equipment, man has been able to deal with industrial fires, nuclear fires, and gas-leak fires.

Most dangerous fires under this category are nuclear and gas fires. This is because most gases are colorless. And even with their smell, the source of fires from gas leaks are usually not easy to trace. And once the fire is ignited, it rapidly spreads, following the trail of the gas.

Although nuclear energy is considered clean energy, it is known to leave devastating consequences when it erupts. The radiation it releases leads to many deaths and birth defects in man, birds, marine life, and animal populations, even with efforts at containment or remediation.

C). Arson.

Arsons are usually traceable to deliberate human actions. Arson is the criminal act of intentionally setting fire on self (known as immolation), or on other people's property. It is the willful act of causing destruction for vengeful, personal, religious, or political reasons. This wicked act deprives others of their rights.

It is a nefarious act by the malicious, the wicked, or mentally ill, who engage in this mischief to satisfy their evil urge. Arsonists have no regard for other human lives, property, or rights. And in some cases, the arsonists have been trapped in the fire, leaving them horribly burned.

Arson creates perilous situations that are extremely concerning. When government offices are torched, vital documents are lost. When the organization known as Islamic State of Iraq and Syria (ISIS), a Sunni jihadist group, firebombed the ancient city of Palmyra in Syria, valuable items gathered over several centuries were destroyed.

Many ancient archeological sites belonging to both Christian and Moslem religions were laid to waste in that nefarious act. Relevant cultural artifacts were destroyed, libraries were demolished, useful books set ablaze, and irreplaceable materials were wasted by this violent group.

In ancient times, kings burned their enemies in public stakes. This wicked, inhumane, and horrific means was the general method of punishment meted out to the early Christian converts who refused to recant their faith. Failure to recant the faith was deemed an afront to the king or Emperor and was not dealt with nicely.

One of the most painful persecutions against the early church was the sad event of AD 94. This horrific act was perpetrated by the Roman tyrant, Emperor Flavius Domitian who threw the elderly Apostle John into a cauldron of boiling oil for preaching the gospel and publicly condemning pagan worship.

And after the ruthless dictator saw that the righteous apostle John would not die in that fire, because God miraculously preserved him, he banished the Apostle to the island of Patmos. It was while on this island that the apostle received the amazing visions of the apocalypse which is known in the Bible as "Revelation".

The enemy's objective is always to intimidate and scare God's children who try to spread the gospel in territories that the Devil consider his own. Fire has great benefits. But it also has the potential to destroy life and property. The Devil knows this, and he never hesitates to employ the evil power of fire to do his bidding.

Human wickedness will cause a man to use fire for his disgusting purposes not minding the horror and revulsion it causes. In ancient Canaanite era, roasting live human beings in the fire, as sacrifice to the gods, or just to satisfy the personal ego of the ruling elite was in vogue.

In that dark epoch, child sacrifice was very common. Kings routinely burned their sons in fire, either before battles to appease the gods, or after a war just to celebrate the victories. That medieval era was so corrupt that men sacrificed their children in the arms of idols such as Moloch (also known as Molech).

So, it was not a big deal for a heathen ruler like king Nebuchadnezzar to cast three innocent, young Jewish boys (Hananiah, Mishael, and Azariah) into a fiery oven, because they refused to bow and worship the idol he made. That was one of the ways wicked powers enjoyed their past-time.

D). Controlled fires.

Man has always relied on the power of fire since its discovery in ancient times. Human ancestors often sat around clay firepots warming themselves, sharing folktales, and strengthening their social networks. And in modern times, furnaces heated by wood, oil, or gas, are in use for supplying heat to many homes.

Fire can be dangerous if uncontrolled. The flames of unchecked fire will leave a person or property in charred ruins in the event of any accident. Many people who are lucky to survive domestic or industrial fire accidents have lived with the horror of irreversible scars that tell their story.

Unrestrained human emotions are metaphorically dubbed the "uncontrolled fire" of the soul. When a person lets his emotions run riot, it can cause irreversible damage to his soul and that of his victims. That is also how unchecked spiritual fires operate. They run wild like an undisciplined mind.

E). Spiritual fires.

The last but not the least in the category of living fires is the spiritual fire. This is the kind of fire encountered in sacred worship or in spiritual warfare. It is supernatural in origin and mysterious in action. And while its source is from God, it can generally be exploited by the powers that rule in the kingdom of darkness.

For this reason, spiritual fires can be put to good or evil use depending on the person under whose control they are. And while not all spiritual fires are kindled by God, every manifestation of supernatural fire is under the control of God's mighty power.

The fiery oven that consumed Abraham's sacrifice is an example of a good spiritual fire. The smoking furnace or burning lamp was a sign of God's approval of the covenant that he cut with Abraham. That incredible manifestation of God's presence was a confirmation of his acceptance of Abraham's offering.

Prophet Elijah operated in large measure by the power of spiritual fire. He ruled the elements so much that fire became a symbol of his ministerial identity. He invoked it in his contest against the prophets of Baal. And at the end of his ministry, he was carried from earth to heaven by horsemen in chariots of fire.

When God manifests by fire, as he showed up in the life of Moses, by whirlwind as in the case of Elijah, or by torrent of rain, during the destruction of the people of Noah's generation, it is always to express his sovereignty over all man and the elements. At his will, all things obey him.

> *"And when he was entered into a ship, his disciples followed him. And behold, there arose a great tempest in the sea, insomuch that the ship was covered with the waves: but he was asleep. And his disciples came to him, and awoke him, saying, Lord, save us: we perish. And he saith unto them, why are ye fearful, O ye of little faith? Then he arose and rebuked the winds and the sea; and there was a great calm. But the men marveled, saying, what manner of man is this, that even the winds and the sea obey him!"* (Matthew 8: 23-27).

Prophet Elisha was a man whose prayer life invoked spiritual fires. He used this fire to destroy three sets of Ahab's captains of fifties and their soldiers. And when a contingent of the Syrian army surrounded him and his servant at Dothan, they received protection by angels on chariots of fire.

> *"And when the servant of the man of God was risen early, and gone forth, behold, a host compassed the city both with horses and chariots. And his servant said unto him, Alas, my master!*

> *How shall we do? And he answered, Fear not: for*
> *they that be with us are more than they that be*
> *with them. And Elisha prayed, and said, LORD,*
> *I pray thee, open his eyes, that he may see. And*
> *the LORD opened the eyes of the young man; and*
> *he saw: and behold, the mountain was full of*
> *horses and chariots of fire round about Elisha"*
> *(2 Kings 6: 15-17).*

God lavished prophet Elijah with the gift to operate by this spiritual fire. It was a handy tool to him and a very convenient resource with which he served God. This fire is an endorsement to a believer's ministerial calling. It is evidence that a person has been specially baptized by the Holy Ghost.

Every child of God needs this fire. It sets Christians free from their past and frees them from their fears. With it, one can walk through a troop and leap over a wall. When it came upon Moses, it transformed him to a captain of God's people from his former position as a captive of the mighty Egyptians.

He became a ruler of his trials, challenges, and circumstances because a sleeping giant, in the form of God's pillar of fire, had come alive in him. This fire burned within him and around him, and was a sign to Moses that God had equipped him to overcome Pharaoh and all Egypt.

The living fire of God empowers believers to overcome the operations of the wicked principalities ruling over this dark world. Referring to this fire, the beloved Apostle John wrote to the saints reminding them that though the Devil is a strong spirit, yet there is a gift inside the Christian that makes him stronger than the Devil.

> *"Ye are of God, little children, and have overcome*
> *them: because greater is he that is in you, than he*
> *that in the world" (1 John 4: 4)*

That gift is the fire which enables believers to win souls for God with ease. It empowers Christians to reprove practitioners of witchcraft, and to patiently lead to repentance those who cast spells and engage in abominations. It prepares souls to live in this broken world and not be influenced by its unfruitful works.

That is why the enemy will attack a person the moment he understands that he has been consecrated with that holy fire. He will do all in his power to distract that person. He will test that fire, tempt that soul, and he will even try to negotiate a compromise. If all fails, he will leave for a while (Matthew 4: 1-8).

But the living fire of God makes a huge difference in a person's life. It sets that life apart, sanctifies it, and equips it to serve God and not panic when the Devil growls like a lion. Those Christians who operate by the touch of this fire upon their lives, walk in spiritual victory.

Spiritual fires were not only an Old Testament phenomenon. In fact, they were a more common-place occurrence in the New Testament age following the more active role of the Holy Spirit in the lives of Christians. Thus, the church in Ephesus was described as "on fire" for Jesus.

During this time in history, Ephesus was the capital of Asia Minor and one of the three most influential cities in the eastern part of the Roman Empire. The others major cities were Alexandria and Antioch in Syria. But Ephesus was the center for land and sea trade, and the host city for "The temple of Diana".

As a result of this temple, considered to be one of the seven wonders of the ancient world, many industries grew in the city, producing idols for the worship of the goddess, Diana. This caused apostle Paul, while ministering in Ephesus, to warn about false teachers who would in future try to "put out the fire" in the church.

"For I know this, that after my departing shall grievous wolves enter in among you, not sparing the flock. Also of your own selves shall men arise,

> *speaking perverse things, to draw away disciples*
> *after them. Therefore watch, and remember, that*
> *by the space of three years I ceased not to warn every*
> *one night and day with tears" (Acts 20: 29-31).*

The believers in Ephesus were considered as part of the golden lampstand of the church. They were Christians who saw things from God's perspective. For this reason, Jesus commended them for their good deeds, their hard work, and their perseverance even in trying times.

He praised them for defying the wickedness that was common among the Ephesians, applauded them for refusing to compromise with prevalent societal evil there, and for holding on to Christ's righteousness. He complimented these gentile converts for their spiritual endurance for God's sake, and for their discernment.

> *"Unto the angel of the church of Ephesus write;*
> *These things saith he that holdeth the seven stars*
> *in his right hand, who walketh in the midst of the*
> *seven golden candlesticks; I know thy works, and*
> *thy labour, and thy patience, and how thou canst*
> *not bear them which are evil: and thou hast tried*
> *them which say they are apostles, and are not, and*
> *hast found them liars: And hast borne, and hast*
> *patience, and for my name's sake hast laboured,*
> *and hast not fainted. (Revelation 2: 1-3).*

The Ephesian believers were further commended for hating the practice of the Nicolaitan's. This was an early Christian heretical sect that led people into immorality. The Church in Ephesus had become a large church, so it was easy for these Nicolaitan's to creep in unawares with their immoral doctrine.

The Apostle Paul had warned the Ephesian believers of a time when false teachers would creep in to draw people away from the faith. The Nicolaitan's did indeed cause problems in the Ephesian church. But they failed in their enterprise because this church burned with spiritual fire.

For a city associated with sexual immorality and gross idolatry, the saints in Ephesus were steadfast in their condemnation of sin. And even when their spiritual fire began to wane, they heeded the call for repentance. Believers, as the brides of Christ, are supposed to burn constantly with God's holy fire.

Any Christian that is incubated with this kind of fire will be a terror to the kingdom of darkness and a great asset to the kingdom of heaven. The word of God in his mouth will burn like fire, consuming the problems as fire consumes wood to stubble. This is evidence that God is at work in that life.

But where the spiritual fire of God does not exist or is abused, light will not shine. And those who once burned with Christlike zeal lose their spiritual influence under this condition. The only remedy is deep repentance. Otherwise, everywhere will be in darkness.

Loss of God's fire will lead to death of the church. It will cause the leaders to compromise their faith, water down the doctrine, and give room for fake prophecies. In that condition, the Devil will quickly creep into the congregation to steal, kill, and to destroy souls.

But the fire of God will always leave huge positive impacts. Wherever it is kindled, it leads to visible transformations on man and his society. It is unlike the wicked and mischievous fire that proceeds from the dark world which puts souls in trouble. Example is the fire by arsonists that leaves horrible carnage behind.

So, when the enemy comes against the believer's soul with his fiery darts and spears, it is God's spiritual fire that enables him to stand strong and fight back. Thus, when a problem appears as big as Goliath, the Christian must rely on his faith and fiery prayers and challenge it like David did.

The believer's unrelenting faith and the holy, fire-prayers he offers before and during a time of trial are the garments he needs to put on, to qualify on God's special guest list to bridal supper of the lamb. Remember, God often uses trials to transform characters and to prepare those souls for use in his kingdom.

So, amid any fiery trials of life, trusting God and staying close to him in prayer are two essential factors that can help anyone get through those times of uncertainty. This is because when fire meets fire, the one with lesser power will be swallowed in the process. That is what God's spiritual fire does.

PRAYER POINTS

1) I confess and repent of all wickedness perpetrated by anyone in my bloodline, in Jesus' name.

2) Blood of Jesus' cleanse me from the penalty of murder committed by my ancestors, in Jesus' name.

3) Cross of Jesus' deliver me of the penalty of murder, in Jesus' name.

4) I reject and renounce the worship of idols by my ancestors, in Jesus' name.

5) I ask for forgiveness for all ungodliness in my bloodline, in Jesus' name.

6) Holy Spirit, give me the desire and fire to spend time in the presence of God. In Jesus' name.

7) Rock of Ages, crush the evil fire interfering with my worship, in Jesus' name.

8) Wind of God, reverse the evil fires on assignment against my life, in Jesus' name.

9) Fire of affliction programmed to attack my life, backfire, in Jesus' name.

10) My spirit-man receive fire, become fire, and vomit fire, in Jesus' name.

11) Finger of fire, arrest, indict, and imprison all my evil pursuers, in Jesus' name.

12) Supreme Judge, bring your judgement of fire upon my haters, in Jesus' name.

13) Thunder and lightning of God, expose and destroy the evil plans against my life, in Jesus' name.

14) Fire of God, recharge my prayer life and altar, in Jesus' name.

CHAPTER 2

CHARACTERISTICS OF FIRE

Fire serves many purposes. It is useful in the hands of God and needful for human survival. But it can also serve as the Devil's weapon for destruction. Fire is very inevitable wherever there is life. And just as it is useful in the natural world, it is also very vital in the spirit realm.

Anyone who has witnessed a raging forest fire would experience first-hand its uncanny devastation. It is usually during the summer months of the year, and in the dry regions of the world, that these fire disasters occur, leaving trails of tragedy and destruction as their aftermath.

Fire is an agent of renewal and change in the human ecosystem as well as in the spirit world. Generally, it can serve good or bad purposes. Because, while the Holy Spirit baptizes believers with holy-fire, infernal disasters produce deadly gases. These are pollutants that destroy forests, homes, human lives, and property.

Wildfires are mainly responsible for a wide range of human health problems, especially sicknesses associated with polluted air. Such fires release toxic poisons into the air that have been linked to asthma, wheezing, watery eyes, sore throats, and oxidations, that cause shortness of breath.

But fire in any form can be tamed and made very useful to humanity. In many underdeveloped societies, controlled bush burning is harnessed for agricultural purposes. After the forest is cleared for farming, it is set on fire just before the early rains.

The burning of the bush and tree-branches releases carbon dioxide, a key green-house gas, into the atmosphere. The resultant ash-bed then seeps into the ground serving as local fertilizer. Also, heated soil helps sown seeds to crack easily triggering timely germination.

Many local communities also employ bush burning for hunting. They use this technique to surround the animals, or use the smoke generated to snuff animals out of their holes. However, uncontrolled fire can cause both forest and soil damage. This ultimately makes way for land erosion.

From the spiritual perspective, the word of God is likened to fire. This is because of its power to purge sins. Fire can refine impure materials and remove their impurities. In the same way, when the spirit of a man is refined by the fire of God, he becomes a refined person that is then usable in God's kingdom.

In the lives of such people, there is no more room for evil imaginations, wrong ideas, and ungodly deeds. Those Christians continue to walk in righteous ways that please God. This helps them to increase in their ability to bear good fruit, and to be established in holiness before God.

Holiness was man's original state at creation. He was made after the likeness of God, in purity. So, Adam, the first human being was a holy man who was called, not unto uncleanness, but unto righteousness. But he lost that state of being when he sinned.

"For this is the will of God, even your sanctification, that ye should abstain from fornication: That every one of you should know how to possess his vessel in sanctification and honour; Not in the lust of concupiscence, even as the Gentiles which know not God: That no man go beyond and defraud his brother in any matter:

> *because that the Lord is the avenger of all such,*
> *as we also have forewarned you and testified.*
> *For God hath not called us unto uncleanness, but*
> *unto holiness" (1 Thessalonians 4: 7).*

In ancient times, there were no written moral laws or guidelines. So, sexual standards were low. The immoral behavior of that era certainly laid the foundation of sexual decadence in the present world. And the arrival of modern technology, sadly amplified social platforms that deliberately embraced sin.

So, the sexual sins we observe today did not start with the advent of the computer age. Rather, the internet only exposed the secret immoralities of ancient times, bringing into the public glare the once hidden arts of witchcraft, pedophilia, pornography, and other ritual practices, which only a few people knew about.

These are some of the vile things that defile human souls and make them unclean in the sight of God. Sadly, the modern society prefers the filthiness of this world which incites men against God, with Satan seducing men to sell their souls to his kingdom in exchange for fleeting diabolical favors.

The good news, however, is that God has not given up on mankind. His plan for redemption is still in place as his fire continues to purge human souls, preparing them as vessels that will receive the inheritance reserved for the sanctified saints, the incorruptible, and the undefiled.

It is thus through the cleansing by the blood of Jesus that everyone, born of the Adamic nature, can receive God's gift of salvation. And with the purging by the fire of the Holy Ghost, all the souls redeemed by the blood of Jesus get purified from sinful pollutions, to become useful vessels in the hand of Christ.

After God's fire burns away the log in a believer's eyes, and the wax in his ears, that Christian is able to clearly perceive things in the spirit realm better than he ever did. This is when Christians can bear the fruit of righteousness and prosper in whatever they lay their hands to do.

A). Fire is mobile.

If natural fire is not contained, it can move with blazing speed to where it is not needed, to cause unhealthy damage. This is because fire follows the direction of air and will magnetize to any combustible material along its path. Thus, the sparks of fire are figuratively described as having feet to run and wings to fly.

The divine force behind blazing, spiritual-fire changes things in its path. This force sets light to human souls, waking up the sleeping giant in them, and inspires men with the passion to search for God and his word. This kind of fire ignites the zeal that leads to life-changing human and spiritual experiences.

The Bible describes the word of God with striking metaphors like "bread", "sword", "hammer", "light", and "fire". This is because God's word nourishes the soul like bread, pierces the heart like a sword, will break down the walls of unbelief like a hammer, brightens the path like light and burn in the soul like fire.

This word of God is alive, active, energetic, powerful, sharper than any two-edged sword. Only God can contain or confine his fire. That is because this fire rages with indescribable energy that comes from the presence of the sovereign God who is the creator of the universe.

At the beginning of creation, when God called the earth into being, he also commanded, and an incredible shining light came forth and dispersed the darkness that was upon the face of the deep. And even though that light and its heat dwell in the firmament above, they still influence everything that God created.

"But ye shall receive power, after that the Holy Ghost is come upon you: and ye shall be witnesses unto me both in Jerusalem, and in all Judaea,

*and in Samaria, and unto the uttermost part of
the earth." (Acts 1: 8).*

Without this fire, no believer can effectively serve God. When it came upon the early believers in Jerusalem, it turned these ordinary folks, mainly illiterate fishermen, into fire-spitting linguists and evangelists. This fire made these ordinary men to speak in languages that were originally alien to them.

And most importantly, it released them from the bondage of their religion, culture, and profession, and endued them with power to take the gospel into foreign regions. As this fire spreads, it breaks strongholds, destroys barriers, and inspires men with strength "to run" with the word of God.

B). Fire can be deadly.

Most deaths resulting from fire outbreaks are due to the inhalation of toxic gases from the smoke. This results in choking. And the more the combustion is incomplete, the greater smoke is generated. This is why the smoke generated by physical fire is very deadly.

Spiritual fire is very deadly too. It is like a two-edged sword. It is a weapon of grace as well as for judgment. In the Old Testament, Moses reminded his people that God is a consuming fire. God is a morally perfect being. But, while he gives grace to repentant souls, he will not spare perennial sinners.

*"For the LORD thy God is a consuming fire, even
a jealous God." (Deuteronomy 4: 24).*

Whenever the wrath of God comes down on a people or place, it may come in the form of his fire. In that judgement, nothing survives. This explains the nature of the God's fiery destruction that visited the cities of Sodom and Gomorrah due to their immorality (Genesis 19: 24).

The scripture reminds all that "God is a consuming Fire". This kind of fire is specifically associated with the judgment of God reserved for sinners and the unrepentant in this world. But the righteous people and all genuine followers of Christ will escape this deadly and fiery wrath of God.

C). Fire can be quenched.

The scripture is very clear about God's opinion on Christians who associate with unbelievers. Relating with unbelievers who have no plan for a change of life can bring a person's shining destiny down from grace to grass. This kind of friendship will rob a man of his glory or completely abort his destiny.

In the realm of the dark kingdom, there are specific demons whose duty is to quench the fire of God in Christians. They carry out this assignment using fashion, sex, drugs, alcohol, money, or music as their baits. They employ these tools to attract the attention of their victims while viciously amputating their potential.

The more the enemy can get Christians to remain on the fence on the issue of spiritual matters, the easier it is to put out the fire of God in those lives. The Devil knows that no Christian without God's fire will have the confidence to say, "thus says the Lord".

When there is no spiritual fire upon a person's life, that person becomes prey to his enemies. That is when dream robbers have easy access to that life. Sexual abuse readily occurs in that person's dream and satanic scientists use such victims as guinea pigs for testing various evil products.

The Devil's objective is to quench the fire in church. And his strategy is to do this one person at a time. It is sad that Christians are blind to this evil agenda. Because consciously or in error, many Christians are cooperating with the Devil in his effort to render the church impotent by buying his goods.

D). Fire has power.

Fire has power and is so relevant in many spheres of life. It plays numerous roles in domestic life, secular settings, and in religious worship, that its inevitable presence cannot be ignored. In sacred religious worship, for instance, the anointing of fire is a sign of power.

A prayerless believer is generally described as a powerless Christian. So, it is out of place to think that any Christian can effectively serve Christ without God's anointing of fire in his life. It is this "spiritual firepower" that makes miracles, signs, and wonders, possible in the name of Jesus.

Many of God's children in the Bible lived in the atmosphere of constant powerful manifestations. This was because their altars were on spiritual fire. So, when they spoke the word of God, they did so with boldness, full of power, and incredible miracles followed their command.

This was the power that burned like fire in the souls of Bible characters such as Moses, Joshua, Daniel, Elijah, and Paul. It incubated young boys like Hananiah, Mishael, and Azariah, and made them relevant ambassadors of the Sovereign God in nations where idols ruled supreme in the hearts of Kings and men.

When Moses encountered this fire, it transformed his life from being just an ordinary shepherd, to becoming a great general of God's army. Though he felt inadequate at the onset, because of his stuttering handicap, the impact of this fire on his life enabled him to overcome this weakness and to accomplish his mission.

In the same manner that fire changes things, like turning plain water into steam, the power of God can take a horrible sinner and turn him into a righteous and extraordinary person for Christ. The life of the great apostle Paul is a very good illustration here.

Spiritual fire has the power to make a person bitter or better. But when godly fire purges a soul, it produces a life that can withstand worldly challenges. This is the type of process that is essential to make a man fulfill his purpose and become the person that God created him to be.

E). Fire is supposed to be hot.

The church in Laodicea was the last of the seven congregations addressed in the book of Revelation. Sadly, the message of the Angel of God, through John the beloved, to the Laodicean church was one of condemnation. This was because that church was lukewarm in spirit.

In his testimony about this Church, Jesus chose an appropriate metaphor that the citizens of Laodicea would clearly understand. The city of Laodicea was very wealthy for its banking industry, wool production, and the manufacture of eye ointment. But it had a serious problem with its water supply.

So, Laodicea was served by water brought in through an aqueduct from hot springs that were five miles to the south of the city. However, by the time this water arrived in the city, it was no longer useful for a hot bath or cool enough for a refreshing drink. It was only lukewarm, distasteful, and disgusting.

By contrast, while the cold springs of nearby Colossae were refreshing, and the hot springs of Hierapolis had healing and soothing effects, the water in Laodicea was useless. By this illustration, Jesus drew attention to the Laodicean church to the need for stable trust as against a wavering faith.

> *"And unto the angel of the church of the Laodiceans write; These things saith the Amen, the faithful and true witness, the beginning of the creation of God; I know thy works, that thou art neither cold nor hot: I would thou wert cold or hot. So then because thou art lukewarm, and neither cold nor hot, I will spue thee out of my mouth. Because thou sayest, I am rich, and*

> *increased with goods, and have need of nothing;*
> *and knowest not that thou art wretched, and*
> *miserable, and poor, and blind, and naked: I*
> *counsel thee to buy of me gold tried in the fire,*
> *that thou mayest be rich; and white raiment,*
> *that thou mayest be clothed, and that the shame*
> *of thy nakedness do not appear; and anoint*
> *thine eyes with eye salve, that thou mayest see."*
> *(Revelation 3: 14-18).*

Many worldly factors were responsible for toning down the fire on the spiritual altar of the Laodicean church. Among these was the wealth generated from their famous black wool and dyeing industry. They had also gained renown for their precious eye salve that healed eye problems. So, they became proud.

Their callous disregard for things that delight God's heart, in preference to material gains of life, left the Laodicean church in a wretched, pitiful, and poor condition. Their pursuits for carnal things that had no eternal value led to Christ's call for their repentance.

Materialism had led the Laodicean Christians to become as lukewarm as its tepid waters, so Jesus threatened to spit them out of his mouth, unless they turned from their indifference. This 2000-year-old observation is still true today as many Christians have lost their spiritual fire having been lured away by material gains.

Any Christian will get into great trouble when the fire of his faith is down. Unfortunately, the Laodicean church had fallen into that category. They had become lukewarm. But in God's kingdom affairs, he only relies on those Christians whose prayer altars are constantly on hot holy fire.

> *"Epaphras, who is one of you, a servant of*
> *Christ, saluteth you, always labouring fervently*
> *for you in prayers, that ye may stand perfect*
> *and complete in all the will of God. For I bear*

him record, that he hath a great zeal for you, and them that are in Laodicea, and them in Hierapolis. (Colossian 4: 12-13).

F). Fire can lose its heat.

When a pressing iron is unplugged from the socket of electrical power, it gradually loses its heat. This loss of heat continues slowly until the pressing iron becomes completely cold and unable to stretch any wrinkles. This is what happens when sin separates a person from God.

This was the condition of a man like Samson who was Judge in Israel. After he lost the fire that made him invincible to his enemies, he was taken captive. And along with the loss of his fire went his strength. Any deliverance minister who finds himself in that condition will need to be delivered.

Samson was a Nazarite. His hair was the symbol of his spiritual power. By law, no one ever shaves the hair of a Nazarite. But the enemy knew he was weak with women and set him up with many of them. By the time he met with Delilah, the Philistine, he lost all his fire and his power, and became a slave to his enemies.

The enemy knows a child of God that is on spiritual fire when he sees one. He saw that in Samson and made sure he put out that fire. He is nervous about letting the children of God burn with that fire. And he will not hesitate to cause that fire to lose it heat.

PRAYER POINTS

1) Holy Spirit, turn my life into a prayer powerhouse, in Jesus' name.

2) Holy Ghost fire, bring down the powers attacking my life and family from the second heavens, in Jesus' name.

3) Evil planes spraying fiery darts at me from the sky, catch fire, in Jesus' name.

4) Satanic airplanes firing arrows at my life, collide with one another, in Jesus' name.

5) Shield of God, protect my life and family from fiery attacks from the second heavens, in Jesus' name.

6) Holy Ghost fire, burn from the inside of my body to the outside, in Jesus' name.

7) O Lord, abort the agenda of evil fire generators for my life, in Jesus' name.

8) Fire of God, induce the abortion of any wicked pregnancy for my life, in Jesus' name.

9) Holy fire, destroy the handcuffs holding my arms captive, in Jesus' name.

10) Rock of Ages, crush any tragedy waiting to surprise my life, in Jesus' name.

11) Powers that swallowed fire to afflict me, choke and perish, in Jesus' name.

12) No matter how hot the enemy's fire is, it shall not consume my life, in Jesus' name.

13) Fire of deliverance enter my foundation and set me free, in Jesus' name.

14) Holy Ghost fire, roast every witchcraft bird flying about to harm me, in Jesus' name.

CHAPTER 3

USES OF FIRE

Fire plays several roles in every society. Even during the Stone Age, fire was a big part of human life. It was a very useful instrument for hunting, for heating homes, roasting animals, and for scaring off predators. And till this day, the power of properly managed fire still serves several beneficial purposes.

The heat from fire can be harnessed for iron smelting, forging industrial and domestic tools, and for cooking. In the waste management industry, fire is handy for burning garbage. In other cases, its flames generate light for human use, serve as a signal tool in the marine industry, and as powerful torch for search parties.

Fire generates light and heat energies, both of which resources are inevitable for human survival. Many other by-products of fire have also been found to be very useful in human society. So, not every quality that characterizes fire can put it on the danger list of life.

The Bible describes the human tongue as a fire. This is a figure of speech that agrees with the damage that an uncontrolled tongue can inflict on a person. In spiritual warfare and in worship, the tongue plays specific and important roles. It is needed for prayers, as well as for making prophetic utterances (Proverbs 18:21)

"And the tongue is a fire, a world of iniquity: so is the tongue among our members, that it defileth the whole body, and setteth on fire the course of nature; and it is set on fire of hell" (James 3: 6)

The paradox here is that a person can inflict worse damage upon his enemies by restraining his tongue against them. And by continuing to bless a person's enemy, instead of repaying them with evil, a believer can bring judgement of fire upon such adversaries.

"Therefore, if thine enemy hunger, feed him; if he thirst, give him drink: for in so doing thou shalt heap coals of fire on his head" (Romans 12: 20).

"And of the angels he saith, Who maketh his angels spirits, and his ministers a flame of fire" (Hebrews 1: 7)

As ministers of God and priests of a holy nation, every Christian is qualified to carry the anointing of holy fire by the reason of the new birth and baptism in the Holy Spirit. However, this gift should not be misused, as apostle Peter was once tempted to do. But it should always be used to the glory of God.

With God, fire serves two primary functions. The first one is to bring his judgment upon the sinner when his laws are broken. The most popular case in the Bible was in the matter of Sodom and Gomorrah. There, God released his flames of fire over those cities as penalty for their relentless wickedness and immorality.

"Then the LORD rained upon Sodom and upon Gomorrah brimstone and fire from the LORD out of heaven; And he overthrew those cities, and all the plain, and all the inhabitants of the

cities, and that which grew upon the ground"
(Genesis 19: 25–25).

"For by fire and by his sword will the LORD
plead with all flesh: and the slain of the LORD
shall be many" (Isaiah 66: 16).

"Knowing this first, that there shall come in the
last days scoffers, walking after their own lusts,
And saying, Where is the promise of his coming?
for since the fathers fell asleep, all things continue
as they were from the beginning of the creation.
For this they willingly are ignorant of, that by
the word of God the heavens were of old, and
the earth standing out of the water and in the
water: Whereby the world that then was, being
overflowed with water, perished: But the heavens
and the earth, which are now, by the same word
are kept in store, reserved unto fire against the
day of judgment and perdition of ungodly men"
(2 Peter 3: 3--7).

The people of Sodom, Gomorrah, Zeboiim and Admah refused to repent from their sins. As a result, God sent his wrath on them in the form of consuming fire. This fire destroyed entire cities to the extent that nothing was left, including man, beast, and property.

God will bring devastating judgment of fire when people break his laws or reject Christ. All those who willfully reject God and his word will receive this fiery judgment. The world was created by the power of God's word. So, those who fail to live by God's divine standards will pay the heavy price someday.

Hell is a place of everlasting torment reserved for the Devil, his angels, and all humans who live in disobedience to God's commandment. It is also called the lake of fire. At the end of time, all those who rejected Christ's gift of salvation, but rather served the Devil, will end up in that place.

This hell is an eternal detention camp for all those who violated God's law on earth and profaned his statutes. Hell was not created for righteous children of God, but for Satan and his demons. So, any Christian who ends up in hell will do so on his own volition. Sadly. Some will end there on the day of Judgement.

> *"Then shall he say also unto them on the left hand, Depart from me, ye cursed, into everlasting fire, prepared for the devil and his angels" (Matthew 25:41)*

The Bible states that the present heavens and this sinful earth are being reserved for a future judgment by fire. This is the time when this world and the heavens above it will be dissolved by fervent heat, just like in the days of Noah, when the sinful world was judged by the flood.

> *"For if we sin wilfully after that we have received the knowledge of the truth, there remaineth no more sacrifice for sins. But a certain fearful looking for of judgment and fiery indignation, which shall devour the adversaries" (Hebrews 10: 26–27).*

Every believer must understand God's righteous anger towards sin. This reaction is not the same as evil, human emotion which is the outcome of bitterness. Rather, God's anger is his justifiable hatred for sin. But unfortunately, each time sin is punished, the transgressor is affected.

Another way God uses his fire is by employing it to purify the character of believers. This is because holy fire purges human character in more ways than the refiner's fire purifies metals. Holy fire represents that cleansing power of God that purges the human soul of all dross.

This is the fire with which God tries the character of Christians to prove their loyalty. God allows Christians to pass through this fire to destroy the evil seeds planted in human souls by the world. After this fire purifies a believer's soul, he becomes a faithful saint whose life will not disappoint God but rather glorify him.

> *"But who may abide the day of his coming? and who shall stand when he appeareth? for he is like a refiner's fire, and like fullers' soap: And he shall sit as a refiner and purifier of silver: and he shall purify the sons of Levi, and purge them as gold and silver, that they may offer unto the LORD an offering in righteousness (Malachi 3: 2-3)*

From the occult perspective, fire serves several other purposes. Not only for burning evil sacrifices on sacred altars, but for desecrating human remains after the vital organs have been removed. In ancient times, Kings and Rulers also sacrificed people to their gods on fire as part of ritual worship.

Even the biblical laws given to Moses forbade this ignominious practice. In the Old Testament laws, God severely condemned infant and human sacrifice and even passed the judgement of death on the practitioners. However, several early Christian converts lost their lives this way for failing to recant their faith in Christ.

> *"And thou shalt not let any of thy seed pass through the fire to Molech, neither shalt thou profane the name of thy God: I am the LORD"*
> *(Leviticus 18: 21)*

> *"And I will set my face against that man, and will cut him off from among his people; because*

he hath given of his seed unto Molech, to defile my sanctuary, and to profane my holy name" *(Leviticus 20:3)*

"Take heed to thyself that thou be not snared by following them, after that they be destroyed from before thee; and that thou enquire not after their gods, saying, How did these nations serve their gods? even so will I do likewise. Thou shalt not do so unto the LORD thy God: for every abomination to the LORD, which he hateth, have they done unto their gods; for even their sons and their daughters they have burnt in the fire to their gods" *(Deuteronomy 12: 30-31)*

"There shall not be found among you anyone that maketh his son or his daughter to pass through the fire, or that useth divination, or an observer of times, or an enchanter, or a witch. Or a charmer, or a consulter with familiar spirits, or a wizard, or a necromancer. For all that do these things are an abomination unto the LORD: and because of these abominations the LORD thy God doth drive them out from before thee" *(Deuteronomy 18: 10-12).*

In medieval times, witches and those adjudged as heretics were burned on the stakes. Also, Parents brought their screaming infants and dropped them on the flaming hands or laps of Moloch, a Canaanite deity. This was also an accepted religious practice in Egypt, Canaan, Babylon, and was later adopted in Europe.

"And he defiled Topheth, which is in the valley of the children of Hinnom, that no man might make

his son or his daughter to pass through the fire to Molech." (2 Kings 23: 10).

So, while notable figures such as Joan of Arc met this fate in France, others like Hugh Latimer, Nicholas Ridley, and Bishop John Hooper (a Protestant cleric at the time), were condemned to death as heretics, and burned at the stakes in Oxford, England.

Sin creates hindrances to righteous living. But when holy fire is involved, it destroys all carnal imaginations, completely removing the distractions that take focus away from God. Fire produces heat and light. These two elements symbolize faith and hope in the Christian religion, and both are inspired by godliness.

For twenty years in Babylon, prophet Ezekiel was a Jewish slave. But he was also a priest who served Jehovah as a street preacher to the other captives. In those tough years, he called the Jewish captives to repentance, admonishing them to obey God's word. (Ezekiel 33: 1-5).

And while his message sounded like judgement to hardcore sinners, it was an admonition of salvation, hope and future restoration to many who repented. The fire of God in his life enabled him to experience a vision of the glory of God and gave him a sense of the greatness and grace in the face of life's trials.

"As for the likeness of the living creatures, their appearance was like burning coals of fire, and like the appearance of lamps: it went up and down among the living creatures; and the fire was bright, and out of the fire went forth lightning." (Ezekiel 1: 13)

Traditional use of fire.

From ancient times, fire has served multidimensional purposes on earth. It played prominent roles in ritual worship, both in pagan and orthodox religions of the world in the past and continues to serve in many other religions as means for kindling incense during sacred worship.

Most indigenous societies still use controlled fires for farm-clearing and to enhance land fertility in traditional farming. The use of fire is the cheapest means for burying human remains, while cremation which was an ancient funeral rite in places like India, is becoming a popular practice in Europe and America.

In the industrial sector, fire is used for iron-smelting, and in the incineration of waste. It is a weapon in military strategy, a maritime beacon, and was used by shepherds in ancient times as a deterrent against predators. Even in this modern world, outdoor campers use "virtual" or real fires to keep off insects in the wild.

Every living person on earth has eaten food cooked on open fires or on stovetops. Cooking on the fire has always been the surest way of getting a warm, nice meal. Unfortunately, traditional, open fire, cooking methods have caused accidents and left many with tragic injuries.

Fire is a weapon of warfare.

In ancient times, fire was used as a weapon of war. It played a great role during the medieval era in destroying enemy soldiers and their fortifications. So, in the history of human warfare, fire has served as a useful instrument for winning battles, even against tougher armies that fought with superior equipment.

Even before the "Greek fire" became a weapon of warfare, natural fire had already played devastating roles in national battles. When Vespasian was declared Emperor in AD 69, he commissioned his brother, Titus, to end the Jewish rebellion. So, he besieged Jerusalem in this bid and overran it in AD 70.

The capture of Jerusalem by the Romans in Ad 70 was facilitated because they used fire as a weapon of warfare. This made the destruction of the temple very easy. The fire not only played a major role in burning down the temple, it helped in melting the gold that decorated the temple.

In other wars, firebombs were used by the Romans against an invading Arab fleet that tried to overrun the important city of Constantinople to enable them to spread the ideology of Islam in 672 AD. But this effort was quickly rebuffed by a more tactical Roman armada.

In keeping with the tradition of their Navy, the Roman ships had the frontal parts of their ships (the prows) decorated with gilded images of colorful animals. So, during what was meant to be a face-to-face encounter, the Roman ships spouted combustive liquids from the mouth of these animals.

As the liquids from the mouths of these animals reached the Arab ships, they turned them into balls of fire. This incendiary Roman, military, firepower, was their major weapon of warfare through the classical and Medieval times, until the advent of the gunpowder.

In 1945, during the second World War, the USA used a combustive chemical jelly known as "Napalm" to destroy about sixteen square miles of Japan. The first bomb that was dropped on the city of Hiroshima led to the immediate and horrible deaths of about 80,000 people.

Tens of thousands would die later from their exposure to radiation, leaving many with painful injuries. Three days later, a second Atomic Bomb was dropped over the city of Nagasaki, taking an estimated 40,000 human lives. The aftereffects of this cruel fire-Bomb remain in Japan today.

Before this event, Germany had been known to use some forms of "fire" in military warfare. In the first world war, for instance, they employed the "thermite bomb". This devastating product was made by combining two combustive chemicals, ferric oxide, and aluminum.

They used the thermite bombs effectively against the British during this war, destroying many of their cities. And by the second World War, they had improved the thermite bombs, by adding magnesium to the already deadly components. The British also had their own versions.

In an era when weapons of mass destruction were not under commonsense regulation, America introduced a more deadly weapon known Napalm-Bomb. They deployed this fiery evil weapon-of-mass-destruction during a ridiculous war against Vietnam.

In these modern times, some of these questionable incendiary materials are still in use in the domestic, industrial, construction and military sectors. The yellow phosphorus remains a raw material for the manufacture of matches for home-use, with white phosphorus serving in the military industry for making tracer bullets.

And while depleted uranium is useful in medical radiotherapy, as a radiation shield, and other forms of this controversial incendiary chemical can be used to generate electricity, inhaling uranium in large concentrations can damage the human organs.

And beyond the use of fire as a military weapon, other highly incendiary materials like gunpowder, have found good use in the food industry, for spiritual works, religious purposes, in the mining industry, as well as in road constructions through hilly and rocky terrains.

The firepower of any military determines its ability to succeed or fail. A military with a great firepower will easily subdue its enemy by demolishing its might and wiping out its resources. A great firepower puts the victor in a dominant position where he can oppress the vanquished at his will and by his terms.

This is also the same pattern in spiritual warfare. A believer whose prayer altar lacks spiritual fire is easily a victim to his attackers. The altar is the battle ground of the spirits. A Christian that will not pray Holy Ghost fire incubated prayers will soon become a prey to his enemy.

Holy fire connects a soul to its creator.

God's relationship with his children has a purpose. No man is a spectator in the God's kingdom affairs. Everyone has been called into a spectacular relationship with God that demands personal responsiveness and full human cooperation for the realization of God's masterplan.

But before anyone can play any role in this complex plan, his spirit and soul must first be cleansed by holy fire. Only the fire of God has that cleansing power to preserve the human body as a living sacrifice, holy, and acceptable unto him. Only a soul cleansed from sin can conform to the acceptable and perfect will of God.

Thus, it is through this literal spiritual purging by fire that the transformation into a vessel ready for God's use can take place. In this new mold, "all things begin to work for good" in that life. And through the grace of God that Christian can conquer things that are difficult for the unreformed soul.

A spiritually purified heart easily blends with the spirit of God, just as nickel iron, zinc, or aluminum, readily fuses with copper in the hot furnace to form bronze. Fire in the hand of God makes the natural, imperfect, man to become a holy believer, that God can regard as his intimate friend and use.

But God's friendship is open only for dedicated God seekers. These are the believers who are hungry for a genuine relationship. The sovereign God does not force his friendship on anyone. But he will open himself up to those who seek him for real. These are the people he confides in and on whom he puts his mark of fire.

God's mark of fire on any believer sets him apart for special services for the creator. It authenticates that believer as someone filled with God's word, the Holy Spirit, and God's favor. And though the person lives in the world, the presence of God's fire enables him to live above the world system or its culture.

God is looking for friends. He is searching for people he can trust and call his intimate friends. These are the people he reveals the secrets of his kingdom to. When he found that friend in Abraham, he made an eternal covenant of blessings with him. Abraham's descendants are still enjoying those blessings to this day.

God shared such friendships also with Moses, Joshua, Elijah, Isaiah, David, Rehab, and Ruth, and welcomed them under the big umbrella of his divine grace. These were people who displayed his characters of love, faithfulness, kindness, and selfless surrender, in dimensions beyond natural imagination.

Every child of God has a part to play in God's master plan. And this begins the moment that individual accepts Christ's gift of salvation. This is what opens the door into the Father's divine presence where those committed in their walk with God and who work for God, can become his friend.

This relationship comes with the renewing of the human spirit. It demands the bearing the fruit of God's spirit, and a life of righteousness which does things that are true, noble, right, pure, lovely, admirable, and praiseworthy. All these are made possible as the believer constantly fills himself with the word of God.

The word of God is like fire. And no immoral person can stand or contain it. It is a refining fire with the power to remove planks in the eyes of believers or wax in their ears, to enable them to see or hear clearly what delights or displeases God. Then, he deposits this fire in those vessels to enable them to serve in his kingdom.

God also uses this fire to shed light unto the paths of his children, as he did for the Israelites during their wilderness journey. He was a pillar of cloud to them by day and a pillar of fire by night. Without the power of this light, every human heart will grope in darkness.

By this holy fire, God led his chosen people from the land of Pharaoh, where they suffered oppression, and protected them until they entered the land of Canaan which he promised their father,

Abraham. Using this fire, God strengthened their faith and kept their hope alive, until they reached the place of his promise.

The unprecedented fiery encounter Moses had in the wilderness turned him into the most-humble man that ever lived. The impact of this fire upon the life of David empowered him to kill a lion and a bear with bare hands in the wilderness and gave him courage to face and overcome Goliath.

It is a great wonder how God uses this tool to preserve his people. This fire accounts for the incredible expectation that Joseph looked forward to, and the faith that kept Job alive during his trials. It was the motivation behind Joshua's courage, and the hope that kept Daniel alive in the den of lions.

It was responsible for the confidence of illiterate fishermen who preached the gospel with such boldness that it impacted generations of Jews and Gentiles and turned the world upside down. This holy fire makes an ordinary man wild for God and gives him power to deal with the Devil in uncompromising ways.

It gave apostle Paul the confidence to stand before Kings, rulers, and learned men of the law, to minister the gospel without fear. It gives righteous believers the audacity to speak classified information from heaven which God only reveals to those his calls his friends.

God baptizes believers with the fire that makes them incorruptible by this world system. But every believer must desire this baptism which destroys timidity and empowers a person with godly boldness. A Christian purged from evil habits will no longer respond to the pull and concept of this corrupt world system.

This sanctification by fire triggers holy animosity against unrighteousness and any form of carnality. It makes the mind to hate sin with holy hatred, causes the soul to detest all forms of worldliness, and enables the body to keep sin at a very comfortable distance.

These are the Christians who dress modestly, behave mindfully without regrets, act cautiously, speak differently, and worship reverently. They prudently choose their relationships, and are careful with what they see, say, or do in private, public, or on social media.

Even though the believer is connected to God through the fire of the Holy Ghost, every Christian must play his role by fully trusting God, using this gift to serve him in obedience to his word. This type of cooperation is necessary before any Christian can experience the true manifestation of God's promise and power.

The disregard for the baptism of fire is largely responsible for powerlessness in the Christian life and church today. The good news, however, is that God is still answering by fire, even in this age. But it is only to those, in those, and through those, whose spirits, souls, and bodies are ready for his manifestations.

Fire is an instrument of judgement.

God is the author of order and creator of all such things as love, joy, peace, grace, mercy, and justice. But in his kingdom affairs, the word, "Fire of God" is a spiritual paradox that makes the God of justice, the same as the God of mercy. That is why he is God. He cannot be queried.

So, while God will use this fire to prepare a soul for the next level of his assignment, he can employ the same instrument as a tool of judgement against rebels. Sinners must remember that a time will come when enemies of God will face the penalty of hellfire if they do repent from their evil ways.

> *"Thine hand shall find out all thine enemies: thy right hand shall find out those that hate thee. Thou shalt make them as a fiery oven in the time of thine anger: the LORD shall swallow them up in his wrath, and the fire shall devour them"* (Psalm 21: 8-9).

It is painful when we hear about the death of people. Whether it be death in their sleep, by drowning, by hanging, by choking, being beheaded, ritual murder, or by being burned to death in a fire accident, I believe that only few people would choose to die by burning in the fire.

This can be a terrible way to die. And human life even becomes worse in hell, where its fire never goes out and the sinner does not die. The pain of such death would not be worth it after Christ died to save humanity from such torture. That is why all men need to change from their evil ways while there is yet time.

From Bible records, it is obvious that fire can be a tool of judgement. In the scripture below, the psalmist states without doubt that fire is a tool reserved for the punishment of sinners, the violent man, and the wicked. It is a penalty set aside for the final punishment of the workers of iniquity.

"The LORD trieth the righteous: But the wicked and him that loveth violence his soul hateth. Upon the wicked he shall rain snares, fire, and brimstone, and an horrible tempest: This shall be the portion of their cup." (Psalm 11:5-6 KJV).

While explaining the parable of the tares to his disciples, Jesus alluded to fire as a tool for end-time judgment. That clarification was as certain then as it is today. What that means is that at the end of time, fire will be used to judge all the wicked people and the evil doers who refused to repent of their ways.

"The Son of man shall send forth his angels, and they shall gather out of his kingdom all things that offend, and them which do iniquity; and shall cast them into a furnace of fire: there shall be wailing and gnashing of teeth." (Matthew 13:41-42 KJV).

PASTOR NNAEMEKA C. UCHEGBU

Making one's ways right with God is the only way to escape the punishment of burning eternally in hell. That place is the last human bus stop from which no one can return. But hell can be avoided by doing away with such evil as lust of the flesh, lust of the eyes, and the pride of life.

Anyone reading this book now that is not living right with God has a chance of making things up with him. This is a warning to those who indulge in evil and are pleased to live in sin. The Message Bible says that, "God will pitch them in the trash and that he will cull the bad fish and throw them in the garbage".

"The Son of man shall send forth his angels, and they shall gather out of his kingdom all things that offend, and them which do iniquity; And shall cast them into a furnace of fire: there shall be wailing and gnashing of teeth" (Matthew 13: 41-42)

"So shall it be at the end of the world: the angels shall come forth, and sever the wicked from among the just, And shall cast them into the furnace of fire: there shall be wailing and gnashing of teeth" (Matthew 13: 49–50).

But the same God promises that on that day, "the righteous' (those that lived by the law of God or who made their way right with God through Jesus) "will shine like the sun in the kingdom of their Father". So, how a person relates with God till the end of time will determine where he will end up on the last day.

Right now, God is not executing his agenda against the wicked. He wants to gather all the good stuff into his barn. He is deliberately allowing a delay until "the end of the age", so that more people will have time to respond to the good news about Jesus and repent.

In the genealogy of Jesus, we see many imperfect characters. Rehab was a harlot, Judah slept with his daughter-in-law and Perez was born out of that relationship. Ruth, the great grandmother of David was a Moabite, and Solomon was born out of adultery in the matter of Bathsheba, who was the wife of Uriah.

But in his grace, God took what the devil intended for evil in these lives and used it for the greater good of all mankind. This shows that it is not God's plan for anyone to perish, but that all should come to repentance and enjoy eternal life with him.

Evil may look attractive, but it is destructive and will lead an unrepentant soul to hell fire. But the merciful God is readily available to help anyone that is determined to avoid hell fire. He is willing to steer such a soul back onto the straight paths that lead to life.

By birth, everyone is a sinner, following the rebellion of Adam and Eve in the Garden of Eden. But there is hope for redemption for those who confess their sins, repent of them, and accept Christ's gift of salvation. Anyone who does this and continues to live right before God will make heaven.

God does not want anyone to go to hell. Which explains his provisions for the forgiveness of sins, following confession and repentance from them. Anyone who does these will receive God's mercy and obtain pardon for his sins. So, if anyone ends up in hellfire, it will be by his own choice and because he rejected Christ.

> *"If we say that we have no sin, we deceive ourselves, and the truth is not in us. If we confess our sins, he is faithful and just to forgive us our sins, and to cleanse us from all unrighteousness"*
> *(I John 1: 8-9).*

PRAYER POINTS

1) My prayers, kindle destructive fire in the camp of the wicked, in Jesus' name.

2) O God, rescue my soul from every furnace of affliction, in Jesus' name.

3) Wild wind of God, destroy any fan quenching the fire of God in my life, in Jesus' name.

4) Wall of Holy Ghost fire, surround my life for protection, in Jesus' name.

5) Fire of God, destroy any altar erected to receive blood to trouble me, in Jesus' name.

6) Thunder of God, destroy the powers planning to use my body as cooking stove, in Jesus' name.

7) Holy Spirit, turn me into a flame of soul-winning fire, in Jesus' name.

8) Holy Spirit, alter my routine and make me crazy for God, in Jesus' name.

9) Holy Spirit, fill me with the burning fire to serve God without fear, in Jesus' name.

10) Fire to serve God without counting the cost, incubate my life, in Jesus' name.

11) Ceaseless fire of God, burn in my spirit, soul, and my bones, in Jesus' name.

12) Consuming fire of God, consume all my lusts and fears, in Jesus' name.

13) Blazing fire of God, consume all my addictions, in Jesus' name.

14) Altar of materialism in my life collapse completely by fire, in Jesus' name.

CHAPTER 4

REPRESENTATIONS OF FIRE

Fire is a powerful element. It is one of the symbols of the divine Holy Spirit, the third person of the Holy Trinity. It is the fingerprint of God, as seen in many of his wondrous acts. Fire is generally used to represent the divine image of the Pure, Holy, Righteous, and Sovereign God.

It is the recognized symbol of divine Deity and generally represents the glorious presence of God, the mighty power of his majesty, and his immaculate purity. In the hand of God, fire is an effective tool for destroying transgression, purging iniquity, cleansing all manner of filthiness, and judging abomination.

FIRE IS A SPIRITUAL TOOL FOR DIVINE CLEANSING

Just as no impurity can survive the furnace, no evil can survive the fire of God. Thus, through God's divine burning process, he puts an end to all ungodliness by passing his children through a fire of preparation. After such cleansing of sins, those believers become ready and usable vessels in God's kingdom.

"When the Lord shall have washed away the filth
of the daughters of Zion and shall have purged the

blood of Jerusalem from the midst thereof by the
spirit of judgment, and by the spirit of burning.
And the LORD will create upon every dwelling
place of mount Zion, and upon her assemblies,
a cloud and smoke by day, and the shining of a
flaming fire by night: for upon all the glory shall
be a defence. And there shall be a tabernacle for
a shadow in the day time from the heat, and for
a place of refuge, and for a covert from storm and
from rain." (Isaiah 4: 4-6).

In ancient times, the Israelites used fire to ceremonially purify certain items captured from their enemies during wars before bringing them into the temple. The materials that survived the fire were considered good for use in God's house. This shows that items for divine worship must be certified as pure.

"Only the gold, and the silver, the brass, the iron,
the tin, and the lead, Everything that may abide
the fire, ye shall make it go through the fire, and
it shall be clean: nevertheless it shall be purified
with the water of separation: and all that abideth
not the fire ye shall make go through the water."
(Numbers 31:22-23).

Even the people who served in God's temple, along with their garments, the sacred implements, and the furniture for worship, were required to be holy. It was this type of purging that revealed the true nature of Isaiah to himself. Through this fiery cleansing of his tongue his real calling was revealed to him.

Before Isaiah's encounter with the fire of God he was a Scribe in the royal palace of King Uzziah. As a Scribe in the courts of the king, Isaiah's daily function was limited only to transcription of holy texts onto parchments. But while this duty was a respectable one in Judaism, it limited the scope of Isaiah's destiny.

Scribes were highly respectable people as most of them were lawyers. They were experts in the scriptures, interpreted the law, and were authorized to act as judges. But while they were highly regarded in the society, and served the nation in the sight of God, most of them were sinners.

Many of these scribes were mere religious bigots and hypocrites who did not practice what they taught. They were mostly superficial religious leaders who pleased the king but lacked integrity with God. Isaiah was one of them. But while he may not have participated in their wickedness, he was guilty by association.

These hypocritical leaders had become so hardened by the evil acts in their society that the gruesome sacrifice of children in fire to idols, no longer moved their emotions. The despicable act of throwing living souls into the fiery furnace was now a standard way of worshipping the gods.

Things had gone so bad in Israel that no one cared about what bothered God. The King of Israel at the time was Uzziah. He was a successful war leader who had defeated many adversaries. But he became arrogant and forgot the God who made him victorious.

Under his watch, godlessness became routine. While men honored God with their lips, their hearts had gone very far away from him. The perverse state of that society then was not any different from our own immoral lifestyles today, where falsehood is cozier in men's hearts than the truth of God (Matthew 15:8).

God is far more concerned with the human hearts than he is with their lips. He is not impressed by people who live on clever words; who say they love him with their lips but do not show it in their deeds. The heart is where godlessness begins. This is the place where abominable sins are conceived and hidden.

"For out of the heart come evil thoughts – murder, adultery, sexual immorality, theft, false testimony, slander". (Matthew 15: 19)

"The fool hath said in his heart, there is no God. They are corrupt, they have done abominable works, There is none that doeth good. The LORD looked down from heaven upon the children of men, to see if there were any that did understand, And seek God." (Psalm 14:1-2).

Idolatry is one of the worst forms of immorality. It is a sign of gross human disrespect for the Almighty God. It is a practice he does not condone and as such, he does not spare those who practice this unrighteousness. No one can truly glorify God unless he considers him as sovereign and above other gods.

During the reign of King Uzziah, this unrighteous habit had become chronic. The spiritual life of nation of Israel was under such putrid water that it grieved the heart of God. Yet God kept searching for someone to send to his people, if perhaps they would repent.

Israel prospered enormously under the rulership of King Uzziah. His reign was the height of Judah's political and economic growth, and this was because of his loyalty to Jehovah. But as time went by, his successes, accomplishments, and victories got into his head as pride possessed his soul.

And at one point during the latter days of his reign, the King attempted to violate God's law by burning incense on the temple altar. This sacred assignment was a duty specifically reserved for the priests, the descendants of Aaron who stepped in and restrained him (Numbers 18: 7).

King Uzziah became very angry because the priests had restrained him from usurping their duty and from defiling the altar of God of Abraham. In the process, the king was miraculously struck with leprosy. This sickness kept him away from the temple until his death. So, his son Jotham continued to rule in his place.

The penalty for desecrating God's altar was death. And because the attempt by King Uzziah, who was not an ordained priest, to burn incense (a foreign fire), on the temple altar, was equivalent to such defilement, God struck him with leprosy, a consuming disease of the skin that burnt like fire.

Originally, King Uzziah was a brilliant military commander who had many victories. He started well, but when pride possessed his soul, he fell from fame to shame. From that time, God sought for and found a person he could use to bring back the heart of the people to himself.

That man was Isaiah, a scribe. But God cannot use a person until he has broken and transformed that individual. Isaiah's experience required that he pass through the furnace of God's transformation. It was for this reason that he had an encounter that changed his life forever.

This is why everyone needs regular spiritual purification. A cleansing of this nature is not only designed for the lips but carries out a purging of the heart to purify it. This transforms lives and turns believers into reliable tools that are usable in the hand of God.

In the year that King Uzziah died", Isaiah had a profound fiery encounter that revealed God's real purpose for his life. This event was probably a vision. But what Isaiah saw and heard bewildered him. It literally opened his eyes to observe angelic worship in heaven.

> *"In the year that king Uzziah died I saw also the LORD sitting upon a throne, high and lifted up, and his train filled the temple. Above it stood the seraphims: each one had six wings; with twain he covered his face, and with twain he covered his feet, and with twain he did fly. And one cried unto another, and said, Holy, holy, holy, is the LORD of hosts: the whole earth is full of his glory.*

> *And the posts of the door moved at the voice of him*
> *that cried, and the house was filled with smoke.*
> *Then said I, Woe is me! for I am undone; because I*
> *am a man of unclean lips, and I dwell in the midst*
> *of a people of unclean lips: for mine eyes have seen*
> *the King, the LORD of hosts" (Isaiah 6: 1-5).*

> *"For thou, O God, hast proved us: thou hast tried*
> *us, as silver is tried.*
> *Thou broughtest us into the net; thou laidst*
> *affliction upon our loins Thou hast caused men*
> *to ride over our heads; we went through fire and*
> *through water: but thou broughtest us out into a*
> *wealthy place." (Psalms 66: 10-12).*

The glorious worship in heaven which Isaiah observed, coupled with the perfect purity that surrounded God's holy throne impacted him so much it revealed his own human inadequacies. And the more he beheld that purity, the more aware he became of the hopelessness of his unrighteousness.

And as he sat there beholding the face of God, and listening to the endless cries of Holy, Holy, Holy, by angels, he realized how unclean he was. So, he began to confess his sins. It enabled him to receive forgiveness and accept the true call of God upon his life.

This continued, until one of the seraphim touched his lips with a live burning coal taken from the altar of God. At this point, a cleansing by fire purged him of his iniquity and brought him forgiveness of his sins. This singular act led to the permanent transformation of his character, life, and ministry (Isaiah 6: 6-8).

From then on, Isaiah's assignment to the people of Israel became clearer to him. He went beyond just transcribing religious texts, to becoming God's prophet. And for the rest of his life, God used him as a powerful voice warning the people of their godlessness and revealing the consequences of sin to them.

Before this encounter, the children of Israel had fallen so far away from God that no one cared any more what bothered him. So, from the onset of Isaiah's call, he knew that his ministry was to a stubborn, unrepentant people. A people that had sold their souls to the Devil to do evil.

But this did not deter the fresh, fire-refined mouthpiece of God. Instead, God's tip that the people will not repent emboldened him to confront them. Rather, than weaken him, it strengthened him as he fearlessly began to preach about a holy God who alone is perfect in Justice as well as in mercy.

The fire of God transforms souls and brings forgiveness of sins. It produces righteousness in lives removing all filthiness that separate human souls from God. No one can challenge sin without the help of God's Holy Spirit. But with this cleansing, a person becomes ripe to confront sin and deliver the sinner.

> *"Surely, he hath borne our griefs, and carried our sorrows: yet we did esteem him stricken, smitten of God, and afflicted. But he was wounded for our transgressions, he was bruised for our iniquities: the chastisement of our peace was upon him; and with his stripes we are healed." (Isaiah 53: 4-5).*

> *"Yet it pleased the LORD to bruise him; he hath put him to grief: when thou shalt make his soul an offering for sin, he shall see his seed, he shall prolong his days, and the pleasure of the LORD shall prosper in his hand. He shall see of the travail of his soul and shall be satisfied: by his knowledge shall my righteous servant justify many; for he shall bear their iniquities." (Isaiah 53: 10-11).*

Isaiah was purged by fire to prepare him for his assignment. And after that, he became a more useful vessel for God and served the nation better than he did, working for the king. He operated by higher supernatural power than most of his contemporaries and wrote about the incarnation of Jesus more than any of them.

His ministry spanned over the reign of five Kings of Judah. These were Uzziah, Jotham, Ahaz, Hezekiah, and Manasseh. Today, Bible scholars consider him as one of the greatest Old Testament prophets for his consistent message of judgement and hope. And he is quoted fifty times in the New Testament.

FIRE SYMBOLIZES POWER.

In the Old Testament, the Prophet Jeremiah spoke of the influence of God's word on his life. He testified that the word of God affected his spirit, soul, and body, in a way he could not resist it. To him, God's word was like fire in his heart; shut up in his bones. And this was the source of his strength.

The word of God burned so intensely in Jeremiah's bones that he could not hold back from declaring it even when he did not feel like. In normal life, no one on fire can remain calm. A sick child with fever will cry unstoppably, and an adult caught up in burning flames will scream for help.

Human fire will destroy a person. But God's fire will purge a sinful soul, transform, and remake him for better purpose. When this fire burns in a person's soul, he will serve God boldly. It was a good problem to Jeremiah that made him restless and caused him to cry out bitterly against sin.

And even though it brought him many persecutions, it made him a stronger person. It emboldened him to relentlessly proclaim the truth of God's word. And even as it grieved his heart that no one wanted to hear it, he continued to speak the true word of God to them at the risk of his life.

"O Lord, thou hast deceived me, and I was deceived; thou art stronger than I, and hast prevailed: I am in derision daily, every one mocketh me. For since I spake, I cried out, I cried violence and spoil; because the word of the Lord was made a reproach unto me, and a derision, daily. Then I said, I will not make mention of him, nor speak any more in his name. But his word was in mine heart as a burning fire shut up in my bones, and I was weary with forbearing, and I could not stay" (Jeremiah 20: 7-9).

There were occasions in Jeremiah's life when he chose not to speak in God's name. But at such times, God's word became like fire trapped in his bones. And this would continue until he proclaimed it. It is a great tragedy to be anointed by the power of God's fire and refuse to speak his word.

The fire of God compels true converts to spread the gospel no matter the risk or the results. Its truth inspired Jeremiah. And though he was derided before his people, became their daily object of gossip, was hated by the high and mighty and treated as the scum of his society, he stood his ground.

Naturally, there were times when Jeremiah felt humiliated, frustrated, and abandoned. Yet, he continued to proclaim God's word steadfastly and faithfully. And God never ceased to sustain him. Both the Psalmist and prophet Ezekiel were in despair at some time in their ministries too. But God's fire sustained them.

"All they that see me laugh me to scorn: they shoot out the lip, they shake the head, saying, He trusted on the Lord that he would deliver him: let him deliver him, seeing he delighted in him" (Psalm 22: 7-8).

*"So, the spirit lifted me up, and took me away,
and I went in bitterness, in the heat of my spirit;
but the hand of the LORD was strong upon me"
(Ezekiel 3: 14).*

The peoples' sins had gone beyond redemption. The souls of God's children had become cold towards him. The nation was literally dead, yet the people did not bother about their spiritual condition. This made Jeremiah bitter. Yet his anger was not against God, but against the spiritual deadness of the peoples' hearts.

The nation of Israel long rejected the warnings of prophet Jeremiah and by this time had been carried into exile. And now, another chosen vessel of God, filled with the firepower of God's word was there to give them a similar message. Yet they would not listen because their souls were sold to iniquity.

Ezekiel was a spiritual watchman of his generation, like prophet Jeremiah and others in that mold. God baptizes such people with the fire of vision and gives them the boldness to carry out their assignments. So, even in the moments of their grief, bitterness, and frustration, God stands with them.

Samson was a Nazarite from the tribe of Dan. He was a Judge over the people of Israel during the turbulent years before they had any Kings in the land. And because the fire of God burned greatly in his life from the time of his birth, he was able to withstand the Philistines, the arch enemies of God's children.

With his bare hands, he once slaughtered a lion, and with the jawbone of an ass, he killed a thousand men of his enemies. And though he won many victories for Israel because of God's supernatural power upon his life, he died with his enemies after he embraced a life of pride, disobedience, and immorality.

Pride was the major reason for his fall. He thought he had become invincible because of his escapades. He failed to realize that the grace of God was the reason for all his victories. However, God still used him despite his human weaknesses, to subdue the haters of God.

No one is perfect before God. And in some cases, God has used the imperfections in man to prove his sovereign nature. So, when he anoints a person with his divine fire, he uses such humans to accomplish his purpose. He stands by them till the end and never abandons them.

God's fiery word in the mouth of a believer generates divine power. With this kind of power, the natural man can connect with the supernatural realm and get astounding results. That is how miraculous signs, and wonders are brought into being.

Consider the life of Abraham. He was an ordinary man by nature. But he was a different kind of believer whose faith delighted God. So, he was filled with this fire that sets men apart for God. And with this burning fire and faith, heaven always responded to his prayers.

On the matter of the corrupt cities of Sodom and Gomorrah, he interceded, pleaded, and negotiated with God to spare the destruction of these sinful people, if he could find ten righteous persons there. God accepted his plea, but the number of the righteous in those cities did not add up. (Genesis 18: 16-33).

A man like Moses was also filled with this kind of power. Thus, when God was about to destroy the grumbling nation of Israel during their wilderness journey, he stepped into the gap. His gentle and selfless persuasions caused God to change his mind. This fire made him operate at supernatural dimensions.

> *"And Moses besought the LORD his God, and said, LORD, why doth thy wrath wax hot against thy people, which thou hast brought forth out of the land of Egypt with great power, and with a mighty hand? Wherefore should the Egyptians speak, and say, For mischief did he bring them out, to slay them in the mountains, and to consume them from the face of the earth? Turn from thy fierce wrath, and repent of this evil*

against thy people. Remember Abraham, Isaac, and Israel, thy servants, to whom thou swarest by thine own self, and saidst unto them, I will multiply your seed as the stars of heaven, and all this land that I have spoken of will I give unto your seed, and they shall inherit it forever. And the LORD repented of the evil which he thought to do unto his people" (Exodus 32: 11-14).

"God is not a man, that he should lie; neither the son of man, that he should repent: hath he said, and shall he not do it? or hath he spoken, and shall he not make it good?" (Numbers 23: 19).

The mystery illustrated by these two seemingly opposing scriptures reveals that a child of God filled with his fire, can operate at dimensions of knowledge, wisdom, and understanding beyond human level. This fire puts them in the position where they can work with God to bring his perfect will into effect.

The fire upon the life of Moses caused God to open his will to him. It is a paradox to say that God changed his mind; meaning that he repented, or at least relented from carrying out his plan. But a natural man baptized with this fire can negotiate with God. And this was what Moses did.

People like Moses deeply know the word of God. He understood that God cannot sin, and so, will not break his promise. So, when Israel sinned and God muted the idea of wiping them out, Moses understood that God will not do what was outside his plan. So, Moses wisely reminded him of his unchanging will.

It was not like God forgot his word to Abraham or was attempting to renege of his promise to Jacob. His thoughts for his children are always good and not evil. But sometimes God tries those he trusts with his "treasures", to see how they deal with the weaker vessels he puts under their charge.

Moses walked closely with God, and God testified of his selflessness and humility. Thus, each time he prayed, heaven quickly responded and did exactly what he desired. Heaven always recognizes the voices of God's children that are filled with the fire from above.

Jesus was another person who, in his humanity, was filled by this fire. His soul was always on fire as he preached the gospel, saved souls, healed the sick, and delivered those bound by foul spirits. This fire burned so much in his life that, even from the cross, he showed compassion to sinners and forgave his adversaries.

However, being empowered by this spiritual fire does not mean that God will exclude such anointed persons from experiencing any challenges in life. In all cases, human trials are part of every faithful child of God's walk with him and the work they do for his kingdom.

Thus, fire can also signify affliction, whether from God or from the Devil. But while satanic fire portends danger, a glowing lamp generally represents a way out of trouble. It is a great sign of hope, signifying that victory or a long-awaited breakthrough is near.

So, not all fires represent destruction. God may allow a believer to pass through the fire of affliction to purge that life, refine it, and then put it to use. This way, the impurities that hinder the manifestation of divine potentials are taken out to make way for the expression of divine power.

FIRE SYMBOLIZES GOD'S PRESENCE.

It is a wonderful experience to dwell in the presence of God. This privilege brings overwhelming joy to anyone whose spirit is connected to the Spirit of God. But to have this special access into God's divine presence, all sins must be taken out of the way.

God dwells amid a holy fire. And before any believer can get near the throne of grace, he must be sure that his sins have been purged with the Holy fire of God. This baptism by fire enables intimate friendship with Jesus thereby creating very easy access into the presence of the All-Sufficient God.

> *"I indeed baptize you with water unto repentance. but he that cometh after me is mightier than I, whose shoes I am not worthy to bear: he shall baptize you with the Holy Ghost, and with fire:"* *(Matthew 3: 11).*

> *"Let us therefore come boldly unto the throne of grace, that we may obtain mercy, and find grace to help in time of need." (Hebrews 4: 16).*

Fire represents an endorsement of human relationship with God. Thus, when God decided to cut a covenant with Abraham, he asked him to bring an offering. As a sign of the approval of Abraham's offering, God's presence passed through that sacrifice in the form of a burning lamp and smoking furnace.

Other keys into God's presence consist primarily of prayer, thanksgiving, uplifting praise, and unshaken confidence, which is faith. A believer armed with these spiritual tools will easily break through barriers and make his way into the presence of the Sovereign God.

The Almighty God is always in complete control of all situations in every sphere of life. And those who want to be in control, like he does, must understand that the mystery of overcoming human problems lies in being in God's presence. This is where the fire to deal with problems and receive solutions, resides.

FIRE CAN BE A WEAPON OF DIVINE JUDGEMENT.

The story of Sodom and Gomorrah is a good case study of God's use of fire as a tool of punishment for human sin. The infamous history of these two cities can be found in the book of Genesis chapter nineteen, even though references to these cities are also in other books of the Bible.

These legendary biblical cities, made popular by their outrageous iniquities, came under the wrath of God for their wickedness. While no sin outweighs the other on God's moral scale of judgement, the immorality of citizens of those cities was so obnoxious that God had to judge them using liquid fire.

Sadly, the lush Greenland that was formerly Sodom, was Lot's preferential location after his herdsmen and Abraham's herdsmen fought over grazing sites. Lot settled in that unholy land, and would have paid with his life, if not for Abraham's prayers of intercession and physical intervention.

Before God judged the immoral inhabitants of these cities, he remembered his friend Abraham and discussed the matter with him. And Abraham, realizing that his nephew and his family dwelt in that land ceaselessly prayed until God delivered Lot and his two daughters.

The psalmist describes what can happen when God expresses his righteous indignation against a person. On one occasion when God came down in defense of David while he was running from Saul, the scripture says that fire and smoke went out of his mouth and nostrils to attack David's enemy.

"There went up a smoke out of his nostrils,
And fire out of his mouth devoured: Coals were
kindled by it." (Psalm 18:8 KJV)

Again, the scripture, says that when God raises his voice from heaven, hailstones and fireballs ring out from his mouth like bullets, to protest against his enemies. This fire is God's weapon of retribution against transgressors and the workers of iniquity.

PRAYER POINTS

1) Fire of God, destroy every wickedness in my heart, in Jesus' name.

2) Every strand of ungodliness in my life be roasted by fire, in Jesus' name.

3) Fire of God, disgrace every agenda of the wicked for my life, in Jesus' name.

4) Holy fire, terminate the authority of any curse over my life, in Jesus' name.

5) Fire of God, render impotent any incantation attacking my destiny, in Jesus' name.

6) Any charm prepared to harm me, burn to ashes now, in Jesus' name.

7) Evil voice mocking my progress, be silenced by thunder, in Jesus' name.

8) Evil covenant holding my destiny captive, release me now, in Jesus' name.

9) Living water of God, quench the fire kindled to waste my life, in Jesus' name.

10) Any oath limiting my destiny, expire today, in Jesus' name.

11) Powers burning evil candles to waste my life, suffocate and die, in Jesus' name.

12) Powers burning incense to afflict my life, perish by fire, in Jesus' name.

13) My destiny buried in the grave of affliction, come back to life, in Jesus' name.

14) Blood of Jesus, quench the evil fire burning inside my body, in Jesus' name.

CHAPTER 5

GOD'S SACRED FIRE

In God's kingdom affairs, there are standards, divine principles, and sacred procedures which God established himself. And even with time, these methods and tools of veneration never change. They are the same today, as they were yesterday, and shall remain the same forever.

The reason for their existence cannot be questioned, and how they function cannot be challenged or rearranged. Their nature reflects God's sovereignty. As a result, these principles and sacred methods receive the highest level of recognition honor, and attention in heaven. They must never be treated with disdain.

The fire of God is one of them. It is a representation of his presence, an expression of his reputation, a reflection of his glory, and a demonstration of his power. This holy flame is a symbol of divine sovereignty. It is God declaring his majesty and displaying his honor.

No fire of God was ever started by human efforts. And where God kindles this fire, he keeps it burning or chooses people who sustain it. It must not "go out" or die. In the Old Testament, the priests were God's appointees who cared for this fire and ensured that it burned without fail.

"And the fire upon the altar shall be burning in it; it shall not be put out: and the priest shall burn wood

*on it every morning and lay the burnt offering in
order upon it; and he shall burn thereon the fat of
the peace offerings" (Leviticus 6: 12).*

*"And there came a fire out from before the LORD,
and consumed upon the altar the burnt offering
and the fat: which when all the people saw, they
shouted, and fell on their faces" (Leviticus 9:24)*

Fires that play important roles during worship are referred to as sacred fires. These fires are the means for burning animal offerings on the altars. Priests also used them for lighting the incense. Because an altar is a meeting place for man and spirits, such fires signify readiness for the conference between the seen and unseen.

Sacred fires command authority on the altar of sacrifice. This fire represents the powerhouse of any altar. Its inevitable presence initiates and sustains the vital orders of ritual sacrificial worship, and its spiritual language is what invites good or bad forces to the altar, the dining table and meeting place of the spirits.

God anoints chosen vessels with his gifts and baptizes them with his fire. But such persons must be ready for the crushing that enables God's power to be readily released through their lives. Ordinarily, oil cannot come out from olives except when they are crushed and pressed.

In ancient times, fire was started by striking two stones. And we understand that it is the crushing of olives that produces oil. So also do the challenges faced by chosen children of God represent this crushing. These trials are ways through which God makes believers ready for the work in his kingdom.

And even after a child of God is incubated with this kind of fire, attacks can come from the devil to frustrate that believer's faith and to quench his fire. But no matter how tough these challenges can be, God will never permit the weapons of the enemy, against any faithful Christian, to prosper.

So, those who have received the call into ministry should not be surprised when attacks come their way. They should rather be reminded that these are part of the routine trials for all who serve in God's kingdom. And these battles come as soon as, or even before, any great spiritual experiences begin to manifest.

The scriptures reveal that soon after Moses turned the bitter water into sweet water for the children of Israel, the Amalekites attacked them. but God did not let him surrender. David and Jesus had the same sour experiences. However, they all emerged from their periods of testing with extraordinary authority.

Thus, when a sacred fire is kindled on the altar of a faithful soul, it generates spiritual light which the enemy fights to put out because of the potential damage it can cause to the kingdom of darkness. The fire and light empower a Christian to operate against the dark kingdom and not be harassed by any demon.

> *"John answered, saying unto them all, I indeed baptize you with water; but one mightier than I cometh, the latchet of whose shoes I am not worthy to unloose: he shall baptize you with the Holy Ghost and with fire" (Luke 3: 16).*

> *"Behold, I give unto you power to tread on serpents and scorpions, and over all the power of the enemy: and nothing shall by any means hurt you". (Luke 10: 19).*

> *"Is not my word like as a fire? saith the LORD; and like a hammer that breaketh the rock in pieces? (Jeremiah 23: 29).*

The word of God is described in the Bible as a fire and a hammer. As a fire, this word cleanses the heart of men, making them worthy vessels usable in God's hand. And as a hammer, it breaks into pieces any hard heart that is laid on the altar of God where the bits can be transformed into a heart of flesh.

Jesus described Christians as "the light of the world". That is because the fire in their lives is designed to generate more than ordinary light energy. And when the light in a faithful Christian's life shines in the dark world, heaven celebrates, and ministering angels are activated.

The whole earth is an altar of worship. And when a man brings his sacrifice to God along with fiery praise, his righteous worship provokes the attention of the army of heaven. The gate of heaven is opened for that believer, and he can freely access the courts of God. This is a mystery.

> *"Enter into his gates with thanksgiving, and into his courts with praise: be thankful unto him, and bless his name" (Psalm 100: 4)*

It is a great secret, because literally laying down one's body, as a living sacrifice on the altar of worship, enables the soul of the natural man to gain easy access into the realm of the supernatural. This is the place where he can see and hear what the natural senses cannot perceive.

In most religions, a sacred fire is considered the proper agent of purification and rebirth. It is recognized as a cleansing force that can liberate what is pure from its impure nativity. It has resolute purging power to cleanse any unclean matter and to remove dross from what is impure.

Sacred fires serve as sources of great change in human lives. Wherever there is spiritual fire, there is light. Through God's fiery light anyone can overcome satanic darkness. Just as the word of God is associated with the light of the world, the fire of God produces both heat and light.

Light from sacred fires provides clarity of thought. If the fire in a person's soul is not of God, his ministry will not fare well as his approach will be deceptive. But when that light is from the sacred fire of God, as it was in the life of Daniel, it will lead to amazing supernatural insights.

The light in the Old Testament tabernacle was predominantly supplied by a burning lampstand, the Menorah. This lamp burned regularly, not just to give light in the tabernacle, because there were no windows, but because it represented God's light that illuminated the whole world.

And whereas the temple in Jerusalem had windows, they were not designed for internal illumination. These windows were narrow on the inside and wide on the outside, suggesting that they were not made to let light into the temple, but to allow spiritual light from the temple to radiate to the outside world (1 Kings 6: 4).

The altar of incense also provided light that shined in the tabernacle and later in the temple, as the incense burned on the fire. The smoke from the incense altar was considered a symbol of the prayer of the saints. In fact, the Bible describes the smoke of the incense as the prayer of the saints that are stored in spiritual vials.

> *"And when he had taken the book, the four beasts and four and twenty elders fell down before the Lamb, having every one of them harps, and golden vials full of odours, which are the prayers of saints" (Revelation 5: 8).*

Baptism with fire.

By the Christian religious tradition, Baptism is the process of identifying with the death and resurrection of Jesus. It represents the literal death and burial of the old sinful nature of a man that was crucified with Jesus and marks the resurrection of a new man risen with him "in newness of life" (Romans 6:3-11).

Thus, the concept of baptism is a vital step in every believer's walk with Christ, and his work for God's kingdom. While the concept of water baptism was not begun by Jesus, he however commanded that all converts be baptized in the name of the Father, and of the Son, and of the Holy Ghost.

This first step as a believer represents a convert's public, willful admission of crucifixion and death with Christ, and the belief in resurrection with him. It is an act that unifies a believer's soul with Christ in his death to sin and resurrection to a new life.

Baptism is a sign of an outward confession of a believer's unashamed faith in Christ. So, it is a command by Jesus, and not a suggestion, to all who confess their old ways, repent of them, and accept Jesus as their personal Lord and Savior. However, the Bible teaches that there are three kinds of baptism. And these are:

A). The water Baptism.

This is also referred to as the baptism of John. This is water (immersion) baptism for repentance and forgiveness of sins. The word immersion, here, is very important because the word baptism in Greek means "Baptizo". This suggests a dipping, complete immersion, or total submersion.

> *"Buried with him in baptism, wherein also ye are risen with him through the faith of the operation of God, who hath raised him from the dead. And you, being dead in your sins and the uncircumcision of your flesh, hath he quickened together with him, having forgiven you all trespasses; Blotting out the handwriting of ordinances that was against us, which was contrary to us, and took it out of the way, nailing it to his cross;" (Colossians 2: 12-14)*

The process of water baptism is a ceremonial act that shows a willingness to submit to Christ. It is a public declaration of choice to forsake the former ways of the world and to strictly live by God's standard way of life. It is also the evidence that a person has chosen to identify with God's covenant children.

Water Baptism is a submission for the ceremonial remission of sins. It is a primary step in every believer's religious journey that is designed to prepare that convert for the indwelling of the Holy Spirit. It is a step that makes room for the Holy Spirit to reside in the body of the Christian. (Matthew 28:19-20; Acts 2:38).

B). Baptism of the Holy Ghost.

The baptism of the Holy the Spirit will only occur in a convert's life who is hungry for it and is ready to completely surrender himself to serve God. This starts with the emptying of ones-self from old vices such as bitterness, holding grudges, stubbornness, anger, and all other such evil habits.

When a convert willingly lays down his life as a living sacrifice on the altar of constant worship, that person's soul gets constantly renewed by the transforming word of God. And as he continues to empty himself of his own will to embrace the will of God, he will be baptized by the Holy Ghost.

There are two forms of this Holy Ghost baptism. The first one is described as the in-filling by the Holy Ghost, and the second is the outpouring of the Holy Ghost. The first one endows believers with gifts for service. And the other type represents the manifestation of the gifts in the life of a baptized person.

Such gifts include:

1). The gift of the word of wisdom.
2). The gift of the word of knowledge.
3). The gift of faith.
4). The Gift of healing.

5). The Gift of working of miracles.
6). The Gift of prophecy.
7). The Gift of discerning of spirits.
8). The Gift of different kinds of tongues.
9). The Gift of interpretation of tongues.
(1 Corinthians 12: 7-11)

C). Baptism of fire.

So much power comes from being baptized by God's fire. It is evidence of purity and endows believers with the power to confront problems and overcome them. The voice of God spits out fire. And according to the Psalmist, it is like the voice of authority that can split the cedar of Lebanon (Psalm 29: 3-9).

The baptism of fire upon believers is a mark of consecration on their lives for active spiritual and physical service in God's kingdom. It is a distinguishing mark on a vessel who is hungry to genuinely serve God with boldness and total submission to the glory of God.

This baptism endows a Christian with the power to operate by an excellent spirit. Even in the Old Testament, men like Elijah and Daniel operated under the power of this anointing. Anyone baptized by holy fire is a vessel consecrated unto God and must not defile or contaminate himself.

When the spirit of death perceived this word, it set Lazarus free from its grip. It was this same authority that raised Jesus from the dead. The baptism of fire helps a believer to fight and conquer crazy situations. That same firepower is still available to help believers deal with their daily problems in this age.

Elijah had both gifts of the prophets and the anointing of fire. He operated greatly in the gift of prophecy and in the power of God to deal with problems. By the gift of prophecy Elijah shut the heavens from sending rain or dew for three and a half years.

With his gift of prophecy, he locked up the heavens from sending rain. But under the anointing of fire, he defeated the false prophets of Baal and Asherah, and all the evil powers in the heavenly places. And through fire-anointed prayers, he caused the heavens to send rain again after a long period of drought and famine.

Also, by the gift of prophecy, he ministered to the widow of Zarephath, and she never lacked food throughout the season of famine. But by the consecration of fire, he defeated the spirit of death that came to steal the widow's son. This kind of godly spiritual authority is a great blessing to the body of Christ.

In today's church, there is a huge need for those who meet the requirement to serve God with a combination of the gifts of the Holy Ghost and anointing of fire. The church desperately needs Christians on fire to fight sin and all the daily spiritual battles that confront believers.

Baptism of fire empowers believers to destroy the works of darkness and shut down the gates of the enemy. The fire in God's word enables a child of God to calm the storm, cause the lame to work, and to arrest challenges from the pit of hell. It represents the voice of God expressing his revealed word as light.

And where this revealed word is heard, it serves as a powerful lamp to show the true way to a believer. Its light will lead any Christian in the right direction, to his God's ordained destination. This baptism helps to expose greedy servants of God like Gehazi and Balaam who make merchandise of God's holy word.

> *"Your word is a lamp to my feet and a light to my path." (Psalm 119:105).*

God reveals his presence through the elements such as thunder, lightning, thunder bolts (fire), flood (rain), and snow. And not only does God's voice thunder in judgment against sinners, but it also comes to believers in grace and truth. This fiery voice that spoke creation into being is still available to believers today (Psalm 29:3).

The baptism of fire prepares a disciple of Christ for persecutions, betrayals, afflictions, false accusations, and earthly challenges.

However, it is a privilege that ultimately enables a humble, sincere, faithful, and committed believer, to triumph over evil.

A person can be saved, justified, and sanctified. But until he is baptized by the Holy Ghost and consecrated by God's holy fire for service, that person will not be effective in God's vineyard. The holy Fire is what enables an anointed child of God to operate in power.

Fire of God makes things pure.

The purity of any raw metal only appears after it has passed through fire. In the furnace, the raw metal is heated until all the dross is separated by fire before it becomes pure. And until the reflection of the metalsmith is seen on the surface of such a metal, it cannot be referred to as pure.

> *"But who may abide the day of his coming? and who shall stand when he appeareth? for he is like a refiner's fire, and like fullers' soap:" (Malachi 3: 2).*

It is this kind of sacred fire that literally transforms a "raw" convert into a firebrand Christian with excellent spirit. This enables believers to operate with extraordinary powers so that God's word is respected before earthly Kings and even in heaven.

This fire burned in many biblical characters including Daniel. And even when it brought him worldly recognition in Babylon, it brought greater glory to God. The same was the case with Moses and other characters like Elijah and Ezekiel.

> *"There is a man in thy kingdom, in whom is the spirit of the holy gods; and in the days of thy father light and understanding and wisdom, like the wisdom of the gods, was found in him; whom the king Nebuchadnezzar thy father, the king, I say, thy*

father, made master of the magicians, astrologers, Chaldeans, and soothsayers" (Daniel 5: 11).

God often bestows this sacred fire on believers to protect them from the evil hands and prying eyes of the wicked. It is like the blood of lamb which the children of Israel were instructed to smear on their lintels the night before the exodus. A Christian who does not "carry" this fire will be an easy prey to his enemy.

This fire cordons off a believer from his adversaries and household wicked enemies. It helps Christians to deal with problems without anxiety, secures them against the arrows that fly by day and destructions that waste at noonday, and enables them to tread upon the serpents and scorpions of their ancestors without fear.

When this sacred fire burns in a believer's soul, the doors of his life are securely closed against spirits of the dead that infiltrate human dreamlives to abuse them through sex, food, and hard labor. The sleep of such believers is safe, and masquerades will not invade their spirits in the dream.

"For God hath not given us the spirit of fear; but of power, and of love, and of a sound mind" (2 Timothy 1:7).

The sacred fire spiritually equips and transforms a believer's life. It keeps him alert, on guard, and spiritually awake, so that he can easily identify and deal with the schemes of the sneaky Devil. It enables the believer to turn his back to evil so that he does not defile himself with what can make him a victim.

It gives the faithful believer spiritual ammunition against the wicked, equips him to take control of his battles, and empowers him to bring the enemy to justice in the court of heaven. The sacred fire of God carries supernatural power. This is what makes a Christian, who knows his God, to be a terror to the enemy.

Suffering is not a good thing to experience. It is a spirit, and no one prays for its visit. But because it goes where it is not invited, all believers must learn to deal with their challenges with calm and dignity, no matter their source. This is because God can also use them for good in several ways for his kingdom.

God loves his children. As a result, when they suffer, he suffers alongside them. Yet, he does not always simply remove suffering from human lives. Instead, he lets his chosen ones pass through their trials. And then, he uses the bad things that happened to them in the time of their trials, to bring about his good purposes.

The scares that Christians bear on their bodies are evidence of the trials they overcame. But the pains of those trials persist when believers abandon God during challenging times to shop for other gods who they reason can help relieve them of their suffering. This only adds evil fire to their furnace.

"The sorrows of those will increase who run after other gods" (Psalm 16:4).

However, for those Christians who give God a chance and patiently wait on him, he pours out his love into their souls in the form of a stream of living waters. This is the way he quenches the burning sensation of any evil fires that the enemy may have kindled in their lives.

As a believer passes through the sacred furnace of God's fire, his character becomes transformed into God's nature. The result of this experience produces a human vessel whose imaginations, perceptions, and habits become more reflective of the likeness of God.

Those Christians become bold like the lion and operate with unimaginable soundness of mind. They are quicker than others in identifying problems. And God reveals secrets of solving problems in incredible ways to them. Joseph and Daniel were two such examples.

Because such believers "carry" this fire for God's assignment, heaven is always attentive to their prayers. God quickly responds to their requests, not to prove how powerful those believers are, but to confirm his sovereignty over all creation through those lives (Exodus 12: 2-4).

Joseph was a slave. His brothers had sold him to Ishmaelite traders who resold him to Potiphar, the keeper of Pharaoh's prison. But a very ugly incident in Potiphar's house led to Joseph's imprisonment in Egypt. All this while, he did not realize that he was passing through the fire of God's preparation.

But he knew God's will, had the fear of God and done some great things in the past that made God to trust him. And when Potiphar's wife tried to seduce him, he fled and left his clothes in her hands. So, after all these trials of faith, God took him from the prison and elevated him to the position of second in command in all Egypt.

There is a purpose for every pain or struggle that God allows in the life of a person. Often, he uses those struggles that he permits to build the character of such people. The fiery trials that Christians experience are not there to scare them, but to prepare them for the battles they will encounter in ministry.

It is during such wilderness experience, while in the school of God's fire, that overcomers learn how to handle the high and the low seasons of life. This is also when they learn how to deal with lack, or celebrate blessings, excitements, testimonies, and the pleasures they will experience while serving God.

So, any believer that is at a low point or is going through some serious struggles in his life, should not let that awful condition have the last word over his destiny. All Christians must remember that it is the resurrection of Jesus and his victory over the grave that have the last word. So, they must keep trusting God.

Believers must learn to trust God without fail no matter the nature of their storm. God will always help in times of affliction. And no Christian should forget that what looked like defeat for Jesus on the cross, eventually turned out to be the greatest victory of all time for all mankind.

Anyone that has passed through God's sacred fire of preparation no longer fears for his life. He is not scared of demons or the threats of evil rulers. Hananiah, Mishael, and Azariah were three Bible characters that God used to show what can happen when natural human beings are incubated by holy fire of God.

These three Hebrew boys were among many Jews taken as slaves to Babylon by King Nebuchadnezzar. Babylon worshiped man-made gods, so the King made a golden image which the three young Hebrew boys refused to worship. So, the King ordered that they should be thrown into a seven-fold heated fiery furnace.

In the urgency of the command, the servants who were mandated to throw these three boys into the fire were roasted by the heat around the furnace. But as King Nebuchadnezzar looked further into the furnace, he testified that he saw four people and that the fourth person had the likeness of the Son of God.

Following this observation, he commanded that they be brought out. And when they were brought out of the fire, not a single hair on their skins was burned. Their clothes were all intact, and they did not smell of smoke. The fire of God in their lives had subdued the fire which the enemy programmed to destroy them.

Moses, Elijah, and Elisha were three servants of God that operated greatly by the power of God's fire. In an epic, high-stake, spiritual contest on Mount Carmel, God used the presence of this fire in prophet Elijah to disgrace the combined 850 prophets of Baal and Asherah.

Also, at some time in prophet Elisha's ministry, the same firepower was also very evident in his life. On one occasion, God sent a detachment of chariots of fire from heaven to assist him. and after he prayed, God made soldiers that the King of Syria sent to capture him to become blind.

The two nations of Syria and Israel were always at war. However, the King of Israel regularly enjoyed, not only Elisha's prophetic covering, but the benefits of his spiritual gift of discernment. This put the strategies of the King of Syria and his army at a great disadvantage (2 Kings 6: 11-12).

So, when it was revealed to the King of Syria that Elisha was the problem, he dispatched a company of soldiers to arrest Elisha and bring him to Syria, dead or alive. But Elisha prayed that God should make those Syrian soldiers who had surrounded him and his servant blind. And God did so.

"And when they came down to him, Elisha prayed unto the LORD, and said, Smite this people, I pray thee, with blindness. And he smote them with blindness according to the word of Elisha"
(2 Kings 6: 18)

Heaven responded. And instantly, all those Syrian soldiers were smitten with blindness in answer to Elisha's prayer. When a child of God operates under the gift of this kind of spiritual fire, whatever he decrees is established by the authority of the word of God he speaks.

In the spirit realm, fire is one mystery through which God expresses himself. He communicates in this language that only those who are spiritually endowed can understand. And fire was the agent through which sacrifices were offered in many ancient religions. That was why King Solomon's offerings troubled heaven.

A Christian that does not burn with sacred fire is an easy prey to the enemy. The Devil will easily possess such a life and use it for whatever purpose he desires. But the presence of this fire in a person's life changes the whole scenario because it makes the spirit, soul, and body of that person too hot for his enemy to play with.

It is a wonderful privilege to be possessed by God's fire. And the Holy Spirit is the person of God that fortifies a believer with this fire, making that child of God unconquerable. The Devil cannot possess that kind of Christian even though he may attempt to oppress him from outside his body.

The Devil does not like Christians who possess this holy fire. So, he looks for opportunities to make them compromise their gift. His strategy is to focus on their faith especially when they are sick or bereaved. This is when he goes after them hoping to make them doubt, condemn, or curse God.

Satan will even seduce them to engage in evil imagination or to participate in other secret sins. That is when some believers begin to fantasize about sexual lust, engage in pornography, commit masturbation, incest, rape, or slide into gambling, drugs, and alcohol.

But a righteous, faithful child of God who possesses and respects that fire will not snuggle up with the Devil. He realizes that trials and temptations are all part of life's challenges. And he understands that any Christian can overcome his trials if he continues in prayer and supplication with thanksgiving.

This is how a faithful Christian can present his body as a living sacrifice on the altar of God's sacred fire. This is when the believer's prayer, fasting, praise, and worship can trouble heaven because his voice, laced with the fire of the Holy Ghost, is recognizable in heaven.

And because the body of such Christians represent a fire-burned offering before God, their demands shake heaven. Such offerings, like the sacrifice of Abel, always receive God's attention. They speak for the believer even when he cannot speak for himself.

Cain was very jealous of his younger brother Abel and murdered him. The reason was because God accepted Abel's offering and rejected his own. But when the blood of Abel cried from the earth, heaven responded. Abel's offering never ceased to defend him even when and where he could not fight for himself.

When a believer's offering is selfless, pure, and undefiled, heaven receives its sweet-smelling aroma. Why? Because the smoke generated by its fire represents prayer from an undefiled heart. So, it sets that offering apart. Without this holy fire, the offering on the altar will not make any effective spiritual impact in heaven.

Fire changes everything in a person's life. And any Christian who has a deep understanding of the functions of God's fire will desire that fire. It sets a Christian apart and makes his prayer life outstanding. This holy fire confers speed to a believer's feet and gives strength to his hands.

After the ignominious defeat of the prophets of Baal and Asherah, Prophet Elijah went up to the top of Mount Carmel and bowed his face between his knees in deep prayer, asking God to send the rain. But he said to the King, "Get upon your feet! Eat, drink, and celebrate, for "I hear the sound of abundance of rain".

Six times while he prayed, he sent his servant to check if there were signs of any clouds. These six times, the servant returned, saying there were no clouds in the sky. But when the servant checked the seventh time, sure enough, he saw a little cloud as small as a man's hand, rising out of the sea.

Then, the prophet's message to King Ahab was, "prepare your chariot, and get down to the city before the rain stops you". But things happened fast and there was a cloudy outburst. And as the King rode on his chariot to Jezreel, the hand of the Lord came upon Elijah, and he got to the city gate before king Ahab (1Kings 18: 44).

It is unheard of in the annals of humanity that an individual on foot outran a chariot driven by horses. But this was the case in the matter of prophet Elijah and King Ahab. With this fire burning in a believer's bones, he will run for God and not be weary, and walk for Jesus and will not faint.

Elijah operated mightily by the spiritual fervor of this fire. Yet, he never abused it. Those who mishandle the sacred fire of God pay the heavy price. Mixing this fire with fake and "foreign" fire leads to death, like it did in the lives of Nadab and Abihu, the two sons of Aaron (Leviticus 10:1-7)

The sacred fire of God in the life of a natural man enables him to do many supernatural works. This fire in the life of Moses emboldened him to face Pharaoh and his magicians. Thus, Moses, who was once a fugitive in Egypt became a bold spokesman of God before his enemies.

The same godly fire subdued the lions' hunger for food in the den where Daniel was thrown in to die a gruesome death. But the lions literally fasted and had no appetite for Daniel. Ironically, when those who conspired against Daniel were cast into that den to replace him, the lions cracked their bones.

Other outstanding characters associated with sacred fire of God in the Bible include Father Abraham, the Patriarch Job, apostle John the beloved, apostle Paul and David. Abraham watched as God's furnace of fire pass through his offering. This was a clear indication that Abraham's sacrifice was acceptable to God.

> *"And it came to pass, that, when the sun went down, and it was dark, behold a smoking furnace, and a burning lamp that passed between those pieces. In the same day the LORD made a covenant with Abram, saying, Unto thy seed have I given this land, from the river of Egypt unto the great river, the river Euphrates:" (Genesis 15: 17--18)*

When God called Moses in the wilderness while he kept his in-law's sheep, it was through an unprecedented burning bush encounter. Moses was captured by this spectacular event that he stopped to see the great wonder. And when he did, he heard God's voice speaking from the burning bush. This changed his life forever.

God always uses his supernatural fire in uncommon ways to draw human attention to himself. Moses was standing on Holy Ground and did not realize it. He was standing before his maker, the Sovereign creator of the heavens, the earth, and all that is in them.

Before then, Moses did not know his calling or his purpose in life. But after God spoke to him out of the burning bush, all that changed. Thereafter, the man who ran from one Pharaoh for fear of his life, ran back to another Pharaoh to save the lives of God's chosen children.

> *"And the angel of the LORD appeared unto him in a flame of fire out of the midst of a bush: and he looked, and behold, the bush burned with fire, and the bush was not consumed. And Moses said, "I will now turn aside, and see this great sight, why the bush is not burnt. And when the LORD saw that he turned aside to see, God called*

unto him out of the midst of the bush, and said,
Moses, Moses. And he said, Here am I. And he
said, Draw not nigh hither: put off thy shoes from
off thy feet, for the place whereon thou standest is
holy ground. Moreover, he said, I am the God of
thy father, the God of Abraham, the God of Isaac,
and the God of Jacob. And Moses hid his face; for
he was afraid to look upon God." (Exodus 3: 2-6).

The children of Israel were in Egypt for four hundred and thirty years. For most part of it, they served the Egyptians as slaves. But following the unbearable oppression against them there, they cried out to God for deliverance. And when God freed them from Egypt, he guided them to Canaan by pillars of cloud and fire.

Elijah was a prophet greatly feared by King Ahab and his wife Jezebel. In his encounter against Jezebel's prophets of Baal and Asherah on Mount Carmel, he invoked fire from heaven. And at the end of his ministry on earth, he enjoyed the privilege of riding to heaven in chariots of fire (2 Kings 2: 11).

In the Old Testament era, fire played a predominant role in the religious and socio-cultural systems of the people. It was also very prominent in the Judaic sacrificial system. In the New Testament Bible, one of the many titles by which God describes himself is "Consuming fire". (Hebrews 12: 29).

Long before God established the Nation of Israel and before he instituted the Levitical priesthood, he had dealt with sinful nations by expressing his wrath in the form destructive fire. This was God's way of judging their perverse and stinking iniquities. (Genesis 19: 24).

Apart from the burning bush encounter when God spoke to Moses from the fire, he also descended upon Mount Sinai in a fire where the children of Israel pitched their tent. On that occasion, smoke from the fire ascended as the smoke of a furnace.

In the Old Testament, most appearances of God to his Prophets were in the form of fire and smoke. Both depicted his presence and his glory. When Moses led the children of Israel out of Egypt, the glory of God went before them as a pillar of cloud by day and pillar of fire by night. (Exodus 13: 21).

God was in those pillars of cloud and fire expressing his great love and power to his children. By day, he went like a cloud, guiding them in the way they should go. And by night he was unto them a pillar of fire, to give them light, protect them from the enemies, and create darkness for their pursuers.

When Moses went up to Mount Sinai to receive the written tablets of the Law, God spoke to him out of the midst of the cloud and fire. The glory of the Lord was like devouring fire on the top of the mount, and this was physically seen by the children of Israel.

At the dedication of God's temple that King Solomon built in Jerusalem, he presented peace offerings at the altar. And after he prayed, fire came from heaven and consumed the 22,000 oxen and 120,000 sheep that he offered to the Lord. The glory of God was so much and filled the whole temple.

This was the first fire in the temple, marking the beginning of the fire that would burn ceaselessly under the brazen altar. At the inauguration of the tabernacle which Moses built, God also manifested by fire. This was God's clear endorsement of those altars as holy unto the Lord.

Apart from the ceaseless fire that burned under the brazen altar of sacrifice, fire was used to kindle the flames of the incense contained in the incense censers and at the altar of incense. It was also used for baking fresh bread that was put on the altar of shewbread daily.

It is impossible for God to permit evil, even though he may allow a person to go through a trial. There is no way the loving, kind, and compassionate God can do wrong. So, when a Christian is facing challenges, it may be that God is trying to get his attention, or to prepare that person for a future assignment in his kingdom.

God's trials are designed to make demands on what he has planted inside a person's soul. This way, that person's destiny is provoked, his potentials manifest, and he is primed with passion to pursue his purpose. So, God can sometimes allow a Christian to experience some pain.

This is the way God works. Over and again, he can permit a believer to face a trial. And just when that person thinks that all hope is gone, God suddenly appears and pulls him out from imminent destruction. He lifts that soul out of darkness so he can see the light and live again (Job 33:29-30).

God's fire makes a person bold.

God's holy fire has unique spiritual energy that makes the divine presence and power of God to come alive in a tangible way in the human soul. From the furnace of this holy fire, he produces uncommon heroes who he uses to turn the world upside down.

This holy fire makes ordinary folks bold and gives them the courage to stand before kings to speak the incredible truth of God's word. He also empowers those vessels that have been cleansed and sends them forth to do tangible works, like Jesus did on earth.

The sacred fire of God keeps the believer's hope alive and makes a Christian to be active in his faith. A person that is endowed with this kind of fire will run his spiritual life with divine speed. These are the children of God who never get weary in their Christian race nor faint while working for the kingdom.

This kind of fire generally makes a believer hear God clearly without any distractions from the world, disruptions from the media, or even interruptions from the spirit sphere. It enables a child of God to look far into the spiritual realm where he can see what ordinary natural eyes cannot perceive.

It helps believers to step out of their comfort zones to become bold witnesses of God's mercy, love, and his grace. It inspires ordinary Christians with unshaken commitment to proclaim God's gospel of salvation to souls in a dark world which would perish without messengers who can point the way from darkness to light.

The heart of a Christian incubated by this fire understands deep knowledge. And where he was a stammerer before, his tongue begins to speak plainly. The life of Moses is a very good illustration here. The fire took such control of his life that he never struggled again with speech impediment.

The sacred fire of God is a chain breaker. It is like the holy anointing that destroys evil burdens and removes evil yokes. It sets the captives of the mighty free, gives believers strength for the battles of life, and empowers children of God with the strength for their assignments.

When tongues of this fire sat on the early disciples on the Day of Pentecost, these men, most of whom were illiterate fishermen spoke with different tongues. It inspired the early followers of Christ to boldly lay down their lives, to save souls for God's kingdom, heal the sick, and raise the dead in the face of persecution.

"Then said Jesus to them again, Peace be unto you: as my Father hath sent me, even so send I you. And when he had said this, he breathed on them, and saith unto them, Receive ye the Holy Ghost:" (John 20: 21-22).

To do God's work effectively, every believer in Christ needs this holy fire. Thus, the breath of Jesus upon his disciples just before he ascended into heaven was a foretaste of the power that would identify those with the true calling to serve God. That power set them apart from others in the world.

This fire reveals a believer's motive to serve God. No one can maintain any deceptive attitude and still operate by the blazing zeal of this fire. And when this type of fire burns in a believer's heart, there will be no secret place for sin to hide in that life.

The fire of God cannot be limited.

Fire of God is not limited only for transformation of lives, ministerial callings, or for judgment. In modern times, it has also ignited the spirit of revival in some places. It is a divine emotion that burns with the passionate intensity of his love to save his people from destruction.

It is an intense fire that causes a high level of spiritual awakening that no human creature has the power to start, control, or stop. Often, it is accompanied by overflowing joy in the atmosphere of overwhelming peace that is beyond human comprehension.

And in all cases, this blazing fire leads to the manifestation of miracles, working of wonders, healings, deliverance, new births in Christ, and spontaneous outbursts of the move of God. It is amazing but true that the God of justice is the same one as the God of mercy.

The fire of God is incubated with the power for battle. That explains why "The Man of War" and the "Lord of Hosts", endows his children with this fire. He gives his power to those who will not turn back in the day of battle, and he baptizes those who are not ashamed to lay down their lives for his kingdom with fire.

Indeed, God lets his fire to burn through ordinary people to enable them to achieve extraordinary things, even in people who are flawed. But the Devil will apply his own fire to seduce the souls of men and women in ways that will first fascinate them, before he assassinates them.

God's fire reflects his glory.

The fiery manifestations of God are signs of his presence among his people. They are expressions of his shekinah glory over the earth, and the tangible proof of his supernatural existence. Though this glory covers the whole earth, only the souls closer to God, reflect its likeness.

Sinners cannot reflect this shining glory because sin carries a blemish that blurs its image. This is why unrepentant sinners' take solace in idols that cannot reprove their followers. Because these idols have ears that cannot hear the cries of the adherents, and hands that cannot rescue those that worship them. They look like God but are not.

That is why it is vital that believers keep close to God through worship and do so in the beauty of his holiness. This demands the worship of God that is in awe of his majesty. When this is done with trembling, it attracts rewards, which include a reflection of divine glory upon the believer, no matter how imperfect he may be.

Thus, Christians who desire to reflect this shining glory should choose to live the humble and selfless lives of Bible characters like Joseph, Ruth, and Daniel. These people were all ordinary natural beings who respectively gave their lives to God in selfless and sacrificial ways. So, he trusted them with his power.

The psalmist graciously describes few characters that qualify a person to be baptized by God. Such people live sincere and wholesome lives, faithfully trust God without wavering, keep their hearts and minds pure, and are determined to be guided by God's steadfast love and unfailing truth.

> *"Judge me, O Lord; for I have walked in mine integrity: I have trusted also in the Lord; therefore I shall not slide. Examine me, O Lord, and prove me; try my reins and my heart. For thy lovingkindness is before mine eyes: and I have walked in thy truth" (Psalm 26: 1-3).*

This is how a person can catch the flame of God's fire and reflect his glory. That holy fire cannot be boxed, and when it is in place in any life, it burns with fervent intensity. So, to avoid being distracted or pulled down in life, fire seekers do not keep company with vain people, two-faced men, gangsters, bullies, thugs, and double-dealers.

PRAYER POINTS

1) Tree of infirmity growing in my life, wither to your roots by fire, in Jesus' name.

2) Fire of God dissolve and flush out satanic deposits flowing in my blood, in Jesus' name.

3) Holy Spirit lay your axe of fire on the root of trees bearing evil fruit in my body, in Jesus' name.

4) Holy Ghost fire, destroy the symptom of death in my body, in Jesus' name.

5) Finger of God, reverse every damage done to my organs by evil forces, In Jesus' name.

6) Holy Ghost fire destroy evil powers contending for my destiny, in Jesus' name.

7) Fire of God destroy any problem planted in my body in my dream, in Jesus' name.

8) Fire of God, pass through my body and roast anything God did not plant there, in Jesus' name.

9) Fire of God melt any chain holding me captive and set me free, in Jesus' name.

10) Strongman in my family circle working hard to destroy my life, be roasted by fire, in Jesus' name.

11) Liquid fire of God, consume the powers threatening me in my dream, in Jesus' name.

12) Masquerades chasing me in my dream, be destroyed by fire, in Jesus' name.

13) Fire of God, make me relevant in my generation, in Jesus' name.

14) Holy Spirit, revive my prayer altar with your fire, in Jesus' name.

CHAPTER 6

EVIL FIRES

In spiritual warfare, two major types of fires are identifiable. One type serves a good purpose, and the other one is associated with evil and destruction. From this perspective, the good fire is often ascribed to God, while evil fires are generally linked to the Devil and his agents. Fire is the Devil's main weapon of destruction.

The spiritual energy or intensity of any type of fire is a manifestation of its source. This explains why the fire of God, the God whose name is "a consuming fire", is regarded as the most powerful fire. It is powerful and serves very useful purposes in life, even when God employs it to correct his children.

Most destructive fires are believed to come from the camp of the Devil. And they are generally described as "evil fires" because of the grim effects they leave behind. Fire disasters have become so common in modern human society that almost all municipalities have "Fire Services, Marshalls, and Stations".

In many ancient cultures, there were seasons of the year set aside for the celebration of ritual fires. This was predominantly before the farming seasons and the seasons preceding harvests. It was during these festivals that ritual or evil fires played the most prominent roles.

Evil-fire altars were also prevalent in societies that practiced human ritual sacrifices. In ancient times, kings burned their enemies or opponents at the stakes. This was also the preferred method of punishing early Christian converts who refused to recant their faith.

One of the most painful persecutions against the early church movement occurred in 94 AD. This was under the Roman Emperor Domitian. He was the son of Emperor Vespasian, and the younger brother of Titus (his predecessor) who destroyed the Second Temple in Jerusalem, in 70 AD.

Following the death, and subsequent news of the resurrection from dead, and ascension of Jesus to heaven, his disciples came under serious persecutions. James, the brother of John Zebedee was arrested and killed. Also, Apostle Peter was put in prison, waiting to be killed, before he was miraculously rescued by God's angel.

Thereafter, most of Jesus' disciples and other converts were dispersed in the diaspora, and they preached wherever they went. But Jerusalem remained Apostle John's main base for a good while, from where he successfully established other new Christian centers, through his evangelistic efforts.

And even though he was now getting older in age, he continued to minister with the fiery zeal of a true eyewitness with miracles following. Sadly, Apostle John's uncompromising stand for Christ brought him mortal hatred from enemies of the gospel, in a dark world, that still pandered to graven images and false gods.

And following a conspiracy by his haters and enemies of God, Apostle John, who was by then the only surviving member of Jesus' original twelve apostles was arrested. He was then handed over to the ruling Roman Emperor Domitian, on trumped up charges of sedition and subversion of the laws of the Roman Empire.

It was this Emperor Domitian, a wicked tyrant, that ordered the elderly John the Beloved to be thrown into a cauldron of boiling oil for preaching the gospel. And when he saw that the Apostle would not die, for God miraculously preserved him, the emperor banished him to the island of Patmos.

It was while abandoned in that barren, secluded Island set aside for condemned criminals that the beloved apostle received the amazing visions of the apocalypse known in the Bible as "Revelation". Acts like this show how the enemy employs the wicked effects of fire to try and silence the children of God.

Fire has great benefits to mankind and society. But it also has its numerous negative effects. These include its potential to destroy life and property. Sadly, the wicked agents of the enemy know the destructive power of fire and are quick to employ it to do their evil bidding. Fire is still serving good and bad purposes today.

Currently, the "Yi" ethnic group, historically known as the "Lolo" in the Southwestern China, and the "Pumi" ethnic group, still celebrate the yearly "Torch festival". In these cultures, sacrifices are made to appease the goddess of Fire, who is said to have introduced fire to the earth by burning herself as a torch.

Other myths about this fire festival claim that it is in commemoration of a "General from heaven" who died protecting the grain harvest of his people. The torches that people hold up during those celebrations are said to have the power to ward off plagues, drive away diseases, and keep off evil spirits.

But like most myths, the only major fact about these fire festivals is their connection to cult beliefs, heathen gods, and idolatrous worship. In the ancient Egyptian, Greek, and Roman societies, fire also played a predominant role in the worship of such gods as Moloch, Asherah, and Baal.

Beyond that role, there is no proof that ritual fires can drive away plagues or heal any diseases. If they had such power, the world would have been saved from the horrible plague called COVID-19, which outbreak was alleged to have started in the Wuhan province of China, where they still celebrate this festival.

Covid-19 was a highly contagious viral sickness that broke out in the first weeks of January 2020. And before long, the whole world was under the burning affliction of this deadly virus. The virus was deadly. And like evil fire, it spread without control, claiming many lives along its trail.

Covid-19 is a natural example of an evil fire. This tragic pandemic of the century was responsible for a sickness that afflicted every race, gender, age, and social class. Many who caught the disease died, and most people who survived it were left with human organ threatening conditions or other negative after-effects.

"Evil fires" are clear evidence that the Devil is at work in a place or in a person's life. When the fire of God surrounds his children, it offers them hope that protection is in place. But when the evil fire surrounds anyone, it leads to death and destruction.

An evil fire is a sign of satanic spiritual activities. That is why fire is used mainly in voodoo practice as well as in witchcraft worship. In both cases, the burning of ritual incense and evil candles are involved. They are used in these instances not because of their fragrance, but to attract evil spirits.

In the religious world, incense is a key ingredient for generating fire. Its smoke and fragrance symbolize passion and love. During sacred cult worship, incense from evil altars is used to generate smoke. This smoke invites demons that cast spells, work magic, or summon human spirits.

It is the strategy of Devil to destroy as many lives and as quickly as hell can swallow before the return of Jesus. So, Satan is deceptively warming his victim's hearts and getting them ready for eternity in hell. He likes to kindle their hearts with the fire of perverse addictions.

Adultery is an old evil weapon that he uses against mankind. It is a form of idolatry. It opens the door for disorder to come into the family and enable peace to desert such Christian homes. The Devil uses this vice to dislocate marriages and set homes and marital relationships on evil fire because then, the bed is defiled.

Satan uses all manner of inducements to distract people from God and to attract them to his camp where they can freely engage in self destructive practices. Lust, adultery, money, and every kind of perverse lifestyle are some of his alluring instruments.

He employs these bewitching tools to arrest his gullible victims and thereby deceive them until he can abort their destinies. With these vicious fires, he warms the hearts of his captives into the bed of harlots. And in those places, he blisters their feet, burns their pants, and ruins their souls.

"Can a man take fire in his bosom, And his clothes not be burned? Can one go upon hot coals, And his feet not be burned? So he that goeth in to his neighbour's wife; Whosoever toucheth her shall not be innocent." (Proverbs 6:27-29 KJV).

The Devil uses several ungodly measures to entice his victims into doing evil. He encourages them to dabble into the occult, engage in voodoo, practice perverse sex, patronize sorcerers, and to traffic in mediums, so they can pollute their souls and become his captives.

In this digital generation, there are many people who still read horoscopes, consult psychics, patronize fortune-tellers, partake in palm reading, play tarot cards, and get involved in every kind of occult activity. Many read evil books, watch films, and wear charms.

These unrepentant individuals have already sold themselves to their enemy. They are the ones whose souls he has perversely marinated with his evil, addictive, sensuous, and demonically seductive practices waiting for the time for their final destruction in his evil furnace.

These strange fires enable demons to confuse the human mind, exploit that individual's whole life, and cause that person to squander his wonderful destiny on the altar of immorality. Yet, many souls love this opportunistic life which drowns its victims in the rivers of sin.

It is sad but true that all victims of sexual lust, pornography, adultery of the mind, masturbation, and all such evil, who fail to repent now, will end their lives in the furnace of eternal fire. In that place, only the fire and smoke of ruin tells the stories of those overcome by sin.

In this life, children of God will face spiritual attacks. Enemies that cannot deal with Christians physically will try spiritual means or visit them in the dream. One way they do this is by reporting those Christians to the evil altar. And a lot of things can go wrong in the life of a weak believer whose matter is on the evil altar.

True life reports of clandestine activities, during dreams, support the idea that satanic agents deposit materials in human bodies which can cause infertility. These have left several men impotent with low sperm count or erectile disfunction and caused barrenness in women making conception difficult or almost impossible.

Sometimes, the damage caused is permanent. At other times, they can only be reversed through a series of holy, violent deliverance prayers. It is possible for these evil deposits to cause conditions such as fibroids and early menopause. But the heat and havoc they cause inside the body is evidence that the devil is at work.

While there are many unsubstantiated myths flying around in some places of worship, there are enough practical findings that confirm the horrible damage that spirit spouses' have caused in human lives. Stories of eating in the dream or having sex with unknown persons in the spirit realm confirm the reality of these activities.

Most cases of intense burning sensations and nerve problems, which medical science treats with no positive results, are spiritual issues arising from the effects of evil fires. When a spell is cast on someone or some sickness is programmed by witchcraft into a victim's body, that person will feel unbearable heat sensations.

Medical science will probably have names for conditions of this nature. It can attempt to diagnose such conditions, explain reasons why they happen, and try to prescribe medications that offer some relief. But these efforts cannot erase such conditions as they may not originally be scientifically induced.

These conditions constitute what are referred to in the Bible as the "works of darkness". The Devil has the wicked ability to turn his victims' bodies into fiery furnaces through the evil activities of "spirit wives or spirit husbands", "strange men, or strange women", who infiltrate human dreams to abuse people.

When this is the case, the victims of satanic deposits through dream sex and food feel burning sensations and bloating most of the time. These symptoms are felt when such victims urinate or make love with their natural partners. Evil deposits in human bodies will cause blockages in the birth canals, making conception difficult.

Also, when people eat food in their dreams from the table of satanic caterers, they wake up experiencing heartburns and vomit uncontrollably. These foods are poisons prepared in demonic cauldrons and cooked on evil fires. This is the Devil's method of attacking the internal body organs of Christians.

Another way the Devil afflicts God's Children is by stealing from them via the art of divination. Divination is the art of spiritually investigating into things that are unknown by nature. It is looking into the future to supernaturally predict events that are unknown to the natural mind.

An example is seen in the action of the king of Babylon (the symbol of Satan) after God turned his back on Rabbah of the Ammonites, and the defensed city of Jerusalem. In most serious divinations, an altar, fire, and ritual offerings are required (Ezekiel 21: 2-6).

In this case, rather than glorify the God of heaven for delivering so great a victory to him, Nebuchadnezzar King of Babylon, stood at the parting of the road (a representation of the cross or altar), consulting his fake idols to know if there would be victory in the battle.

"For the king of Babylon stood at the parting of the way, at the head of the two ways, to use divination: he made his arrows bright, he consulted with images, he looked in the liver" (Ezekiel 21:21),

"Let them bring them forth and shew us what shall happen: let them shew the former things, what they be, that we may consider them, and know the latter end of them; or declare us things for to come." (Isaiah 41:22 KJV.

"For I beheld, and there was no man; even among them, and there was no counsellor, that, when I asked of them, could answer a word" (Isaiah 41:28 KJV)

Idolatry is another way. It is a spiritual form of adultery. It is a practice that defiles the temple of God as it expresses divided loyalty by showing affection to another god other than God. This is a rebellious act against the righteous God who will not share his glory with another thing or person. It is equivalent to spiritual polygamy.

Acts such as divination, bewitchment, or enchantment, are other ungodly means through which the enemy spiritually invades the privacy of human souls to sow evil seeds. These actions are the reasons some Christians wake up from sleep to find uncommon marks, scratches, and incisions on all parts of their body.

Such witchcraft lacerations, evil identification marks, and tattoos, are the evidence of cultic initiations that were performed on human bodies while their victims slept. Some of these visible marks can also be received from being flogged by a person's village masquerades in his dreams.

Life is war and the Devil uses any weapon at his disposal for his battles. The uncommon itching with swellings on human skin shows that the enemy visited his victim in the dream. During such nocturnal visits, the enemy can administer satanic vaccines, give injections, or intravenous fluids, to their victims (Matthew 13: 25).

These days, the Devil is no longer interested in stopping Christians from going to church or worshipping God. Instead, he is using an old strategy. Pharaoh told once Moses, "you go and worship the Lord, but do not go far", "you may go and worship the Lord; but you must leave your sheep and cattle here" (Exodus 8: 28; 10: 24).

The enemy wants to lay down the terms and determine the conditions under which Christians can worship their God. That is why he introduced worldly music and fashion into the Church. Today he uses artists who deck and adorn themselves in demonic costumes to create and perform songs in churches.

Sadly, many Christians enjoy the music, not knowing that the lyrics that "fire up" their souls are the reasons for their self-bondage. These are immoral songs that enable the devil to easily destroy sound biblical doctrines on which believers built their faith. (2 Timothy 4).

This explains why witches and occultists now comfortably attend church, sit in the pews, lift-up their hands in praise, prayer, and worship, during service, and no one notices the evil going on. Why? Because believers no longer operate by holy fire and the condition has made many churches into glorified graveyards.

In this generation, the devil is in his top form creating all manner of problems in the church and making believers insensitive to the Holy Spirit. Witchcraft is now more openly practiced, and it is escalating, while cultism has resurfaced publicly, with occult groups now well positioned to possess the church and the nations.

What a shame that witches have now become prayer warriors in the churches because those baptized with gifts of the Holy Ghost to discern their activities are in spiritual coma. When a church lacks the Holy fire, witches will sneak in, take over the pulpit, and even pray in "tongues" unnoticed.

Because of this, souls in many modern churches are dancing themselves to hell while the Devil is rejoicing. He is using the services of politicians, false prophets, fashion designers, musicians, and influential people in society as tools to draw people out of their relationships with God.

Satan is using his agents to draw souls out from the light of God's presence so he can bring them into the kingdom of darkness to fulfill his purpose. The evil songs, ungodly dance steps, unholy fashion designs, and "Jezebel kind of make-ups, are the evil weapons seducing souls that he will eventually send to hellfire.

The foul songs inspired by satanic artists are designed to desecrate God's purity, dishonor his righteous sovereignty, debase his dignity, and defile the human body. This way, the enemy opens doors in human lives for demons to enter such people, possess their souls, and through them defile and possess other victims.

Ordinarily, fire is used by shepherds to protect their sheep from predators in the dark. So, it is easy for evil predators to strike when holy fire is not in operation. The same is the case in spiritual warfare. Where there is no holy fire, the ungodly will have victory over the righteous.

Fire generally represents different emotional energies. Some of these include passion, love, and happiness. Others from the spiritual perspective include a clear vision, deep revelation, unique wisdom, unadulterated truth, perfect understanding, wakefulness, or superiority.

But it (fire) can also symbolize the power of destruction, like danger, anger, hatred, or rage. Thus, if a person dreams of raging fire in his sleep, it can be a good or bad omen. It is a good omen if the dreamer wakes up calm and unruffled. On the other hand, it is an evil sign, if the dream ends in a nightmare.

The Devil employs his evil fire to cause nightmares in the dream in preparation of what he will do in the daytime. This is some of his usual pattern and he does not readily change it. Above all, the nightmares he creates foreshadow the treatment reserved for anyone that will end up in Hell fire.

The only people who can get away from Satan's punishments are those who know who Jesus is, understand his mission on earth, and know their right in Christ. Many Christians in this generation are powerless because they lack the spiritual fire of God. As a result, the Devil is waiting to welcome them in hell.

In the days of Jesus Christ on earth, many people followed him but did not know who he was. But all that lethargy changed after his crucifixion, death, resurrection, and ascension to heaven. This led the Holy Ghost to baptize believers and incubate them with "the fire" for ministry. Those who overcome will not experience the fire of hell.

> *"But ye shall receive power, after that the Holy Ghost is come upon you: and ye shall be witnesses unto me both in Jerusalem, and in all Judaea, and in Samaria, and unto the uttermost part of the earth" (Acts 1:8)*

> *"And when the day of Pentecost was fully come, they were all with one accord in one place. And suddenly there came a sound from heaven as of a rushing mighty wind, and it filled all the house where they were sitting. And there appeared unto them cloven tongues like as of fire, and it sat upon each of them. And they were all filled with the Holy Ghost, and began to speak with other tongues, as the Spirit gave them utterance" (Acts 2: 1-4)*

A believer who does not intimately know Christ cannot enjoy his right as a Christian. And even though the Holy Spirit indwells such a person because he is born again, he will not operate in the fire that makes believers invincible to the enemy. He may have the key to the kingdom, but it will not be useful in his hands.

The devil specializes in troubling believers to make them doubt God's love. He is an expert at making evil look very attractive and he packages it with such glitter that it becomes difficult to convince anyone that there is something else better. This way, he makes such believers question the reason for their faith.

In this digital generation, it is even easier for him to spread his virulent fire and unrighteousness and so pollute the minds of gullible Christians. However, God anoints believers with the power to defeat his lies. But when God puts his fire upon a soul, it is that believer's duty to use it on demand to serve God and humanity.

So, it is the responsibility of children of God to stand against the strategies of this wicked Devil, his scams, and his lying schemes, all of which are designed to kill the fire of God's children. However, it is only those serious believers that carry the fire and are ready to use it that can do this.

Thus, the Christians that know their God, will boldly work with him, and do exploits for his kingdom. They know who they believe, and he gives them the keys of the kingdom to lock the enemy out of their lives and ministry. It is the baptism with fire that endows believers with power to do exploits for God.

The Devil is a wicked creature. He was not originally made that way. But he became an architect of evil over time because of his evil ambition. So, he was cast out of heaven to earth. And now, his objective is to afflict anyone that identifies with Christ. All his weapons are crude, and their effects burn like fire.

And while he works mainly through the agency of his demons, at other times he uses the services of humans, like he did through King Nebuchadnezzar. This evil King was the one who cast three Hebrew slaves into a seven-fold heated, fiery furnace, because they refused to bow to his idol.

Right now, many human destinies are sitting inside their detractors' fire of affliction because they, consciously or by design, fell victim to the Devil. The good news, however, is that God never abandons his children in the times of desolation. Instead, he climbs into the fires designed to destroy them, so he can rescue them.

God did this for those three righteous boys because they firmly held on to their faith. In the end, their garments were not torched by the fire, neither did the smoke suffocate them. Anyone who can trust God during his fiery trials can be sure of his deliverance too.

"And the LORD, he it is that doth go before thee;
he will be with thee, he will not fail thee, neither

forsake thee: fear not, neither be dismayed"
(Deuteronomy 31: 8).

In the Old Testament Bible, we read of an event that led to the deaths of two sons of Aaron. From that story, we understand that Nadab and Abihu were struck dead in the tabernacle because they offered unholy fire before God. So, fire from the presence of the Lord consumed them.

"And Nadab and Abihu, the sons of Aaron, took
either of them his censer, and put fire therein,
and put incense thereon, and offered strange
fire before the LORD, which he commanded them
not. And there went out fire from the LORD, and
devoured them, and they died before the LORD"
(Leviticus 10: 1-2).

God's fire is Holy fire, and it must not be compromised or used alongside foreign fire. It is not the same as the fire of witchcraft which is used in the worship of idols. By God's kingdom standards nothing with blemish or impure can be used in the worship of the holy and righteous God.

The eyes of God are so pure they cannot behold iniquity. Rebellion in any manner is iniquity before God whose holiness abhors sin. Bringing foreign fire before God is courting his wrath. So, when Nadab and Abihu offered their "own fire" contrary to God's command, they paid dearly with their lives (Exodus 30: 9).

There is a clear distinction between the holy fire of God and the unrighteous flame of the Devil. Thus, every person who desires to worship God, must desire to be like him in purity of mind and spirit. It is only in this context that any Christian can realize his own unrighteous in the presence of a Holy God.

In the dark world, evil fires are used to accomplish unrighteous purposes. They are used for human sacrifice, divination, enchantment, casting spells, and during witchcraft worship. All these evils were condemned in the Bible. They remain contrary to the ways of God, even today.

The word of God teaches that these sins are the works of the Devil. And those who practice them are children of the Devil. In the Old Testament Bible, the law of Moses pronounced the judgement of death by stoning for the practitioners of these evils. They constitute the works of darkness Jesus came to destroy.

"A man also or woman that hath a familiar spirit, or that is a wizard, shall surely be put to death: they shall stone them with stones: their blood shall be upon them" (Leviticus 20: 27).

"He that committeth sin is of the devil; for the devil sinneth from the beginning. For this purpose the Son of God was manifested, that he might destroy the works of the devil" (1 John 3: 8).

The reason God punished the original occupants of the land of Canaan was because they engaged in abominable sins. And when he chose the children of Israel to takeover that land, he warned them against engaging in those ungodly activities because of the consequences. For the portion of such sinners was in the lake of fire.

"Regard not them that have familiar spirits, neither seek after wizards, to be defiled by them: I am the LORD your God" (Leviticus 19: 31).

Worshipping God in ways contrary to his righteous standard invites his wrath. And no matter how well-intentioned a person may be, he will bring a great punishment upon himself. How we worship God matters, as afflictions await those who kindle any evil fire through their worship (Leviticus 8: 4-6, 9, 13).

However, God can sometimes permit his children to suffer fiery afflictions. But these are for his name to be glorified. Thus, he allowed the nation of Israel to remain in Pharaoh's "iron furnace" until the time was ripe. Then he showed his power of deliverance through the miracle of plagues he put upon the Egyptians.

> *"And the LORD said unto Moses, Yet will I bring one plague more upon Pharaoh, and upon Egypt; afterwards he will let you go hence: when he shall let you go, he shall surely thrust you out hence altogether" (Exodus 11: 1).*

When the children of Israel were under harsh oppression in Egypt, they cried to God for help. He heard their cries from heaven and came down to deliver them. Although the people felt that the rescue operation was not working as fast as they wished.

What they did not understand was that the ways of God are different from the ways of man. God's plans are always better than what anyone can purpose for himself. God knows the outcome of every situation and his plans will always bring the best results for his children if they can be patient and obedient.

A person can be in the worst "fire", facing the harshest pain, suffering, or hardship. It may be the fire of barrenness, jealousy, hatred by people they love, unjust accusation, envy, mockery, insults, or miscarriage of justice. But everyone must remember that Jesus also went through persecutions for his sake.

The Devil attacks Christians when he perceives the mark of greatness in their lives. That is when he doubles his fiery afflictions from all sides to shake the faith of those believers and make them doubt God, so that they can be disconnected from their relationship with God and miss their purpose.

From the moment the enemy discovers the value of a believer's potential, he will kindle a fire of despair to frustrate him. The Devil does not want Christians to make progress. His objective is to make them believe that God is responsible for their woes, failures, frustrations, and stagnancy.

So, he applies fiery afflictions to make Christians to grieve, murmur, and to grumble in ways that are devastating to their faith. But the faithful believer can be thankful to God for sending his Son Jesus Christ to set us free and destroy the works of darkness.

Think about what great damage a lying tongue can cause in a neighborhood. And the destruction that swindlers who talk out of both sides of their mouths can do. That is what the Devil uses evil fires to accomplish. He knows that lying and complaining will put off God's fire, so he encourages the misuse of the tongue.

So those that want to carry the fire of God must avoid the things which God hates for they are abomination to him. These include: "Putting others down while considering themselves superior, spreading lies and rumors, and spilling the blood of the innocent.

Also, plotting evil in the heart toward other people, gloating over the failure of those considered to be enemies, doing what's plainly wrong, spouting lies in false testimony against a person's neighbor, and stirring up strife between friends. All these are entirely despicable before God (Proverbs 6:16-19).

Horrible acts such as these are motivated by the devil to achieve his evil purposes. God considers them as abomination. This is because they do not only inflict enormous damage to human lives and to the society, but the Devil leads his victims to do them, so they can sin against God.

Consider the damage just one person can do by stirring up dissent in a marriage. Then, think of how much damage can be done by one agent of the Devil who brings chaos in a family, in the community, church, or nation. These are some of the horrible works of darkness.

The enemy knows every human weakness. And his method is to attract the attention of God's children by feeding on these weaknesses and distracting them with the seductive pleasures of life to make them to remain unfaithful and sin against God.

The instant gratification Satan offers his victims is deceptive and unholy. It is an evil hook that has taken many people's focus away from the fiery throne of the sovereign God and thereby destroyed human souls, homes, friendships, and relationships with God.

So, the Christian must stand strong against these challenges. And no matter the intensity of his misery, trials, and tribulations, he should consider them as the inevitable steppingstones for climbing to his next level in life. Looking up to God is what will help anyone overcome his season of fiery trials.

"My brethren, count it all joy when ye fall into divers temptations; Knowing this, that the trying of your faith worketh patience. But let patience have her perfect work, that ye may be perfect and entire, wanting nothing" (James 1: 2-4).

"Blessed be the God and Father of our Lord Jesus Christ, which according to his abundant mercy hath begotten us again unto a lively hope by the resurrection of Jesus Christ from the dead, To an inheritance incorruptible, and undefiled, and that fadeth not away, reserved in heaven for you, Who are kept by the power of God through faith unto salvation ready to be revealed in the last time. Wherein ye greatly rejoice, though now for a season, if need be, ye are in heaviness through manifold temptations: That the trial of your faith, being much more precious than of gold that perisheth, though it be tried with fire, might be found unto praise and honour and glory at the appearing of Jesus Christ:" (1 Peter 1: 3-7).

God is always faithful to see his people through to a glorious end. He does not forget his people in any fire of affliction. When he does not put out the fire for them, he walks through it with them, giving them the strength to endure to the end to where they can enjoy the reward of their patience.

"For thus saith the LORD, That after seventy years be accomplished at Babylon I will visit you, and perform my good word toward you, in causing you to return to this place. For I know the thoughts that I think toward you, saith the LORD, thoughts of peace, and not of evil, to give you an expected end. Then shall ye call upon me, and ye shall go and pray unto me, and I will hearken unto you" (Jeremiah 29" 10-12).

If anyone will call on God during his trial season, he will be rescued just for believing that God can help. And when God comes to the rescue, he does it in ways that are clear that the deliverance was possible only because of his intervention. God promises that he will not forsake his children. And he never does so.

In the life of faithful believers, God sometimes permits the evil fire that the enemy kindles to make them cry bitter tears, to be the fire that will cause those Christians to smile. So, in the end, what the enemies planned for evil in those lives, turn out for good.

Patriarch Job passed through many such fiery trials. They all came like a flood. And in a short season, everything that that righteous man worked for was gone. Through all his challenge God watched his actions and listened to his words. And while the Devil buffeted him, he never sinned in word or deed.

"And there was a day when his sons and his daughters were eating and drinking wine in their eldest brother's house: And there came a messenger unto Job, and said, The oxen were plowing, and the asses feeding beside them: And the Sabeans

fell upon them, and took them away; yea, they have slain the servants with the edge of the sword; and I only am escaped alone to tell thee. While he was yet speaking, there came also another, and said, The fire of God is fallen from heaven, and hath burned up the sheep, and the servants, and consumed them; and I only am escaped alone to tell thee. While he was yet speaking, there came also another, and said, The Chaldeans made out three bands, and fell upon the camels, and have carried them away, yea, and slain the servants with the edge of the sword; and I only am escaped alone to tell thee. While he was yet speaking, there came also another, and said, Thy sons and thy daughters were eating and drinking wine in their eldest brother's house: And, behold, there came a great wind from the wilderness, and smote the four corners of the house, and it fell upon the young men, and they are dead; and I only am escaped alone to tell thee. Then Job arose, and rent his mantle, and shaved his head, and fell down upon the ground, and worshipped, And said, Naked came I out of my mother's womb, and naked shall I return thither: the Lord gave, and the Lord hath taken away; blessed be the name of the Lord. In all this Job sinned not, nor charged God foolishly." (Job 1: 13-22).

Thus, a believer who finds himself struggling with adversity should not feed the already bad situation with feeling of depression. This gives the devil further leverage to mock Christ. Feelings of resentment and self-condemnation in tough seasons worsen a person's condition. They help the enemy to increase their fire.

Problems are inevitable in life. And engaging in self-pity in such times is not a good option. But by looking up to Jesus when in troubled waters, the Christian will get help from the one who can still all storms. So, when in the evil furnace of life, the Christian is advised not feed his fears but to starve his doubts.

PRAYER POINTS

1) I release a stone of fire into the head of the Goliath standing before me, in Jesus' name.

2) Angel with sword of fire, protect the gates of my life, in Jesus' name.

3) Fire of deliverance, pass through my foundation and set me free, in Jesus' name.

4) O God that answers by fire, answer me by fire, in Jesus' name.

5) Consuming fire of God, devour my problems, in Jesus' name.

6) God of Elijah, convert my tests to testimonies, in Jesus' name.

7) Caldron of darkness purchased to cook my destiny, break to pieces, in Jesus' name.

8) O God, make me a flaming sword of fire that is useful in your kingdom, in Jesus' name.

9) Finger of fire, cancel every judgement against my life, in Jesus' name.

10) Finger of God, erase every contrary report against my life, in Jesus' name.

11) Incense of my prayers, provoke favor for my sake, in Jesus' name.

12) Holy Ghost Fire, defeat all unfinished battles raging in my foundation, in Jesus' name.

13) Fire of God energize me to stay more in God's presence, in Jesus' name.

14) Fire as in the day of Pentecost, burn afresh in my life, in Jesus' name.

CHAPTER 7

FIRE! FIRE! EVERYWHERE

Fire is a symbol of the divine presence of God. That is why undying flames of holy fire illuminate his habitation in heaven. This ceaseless brightness of divine glory which surrounds God's throne is evidence of his undeniable invincibility, his immortal personality, and his immaculate divinity.

The radiant splendor surrounding God's throne constantly advertises the beauty of his holiness. This is as the Cherubim and Seraphim bow before him in worship while the blazing glory of divine majestic fire eloquently announces his sovereignty, power, might, and greatness, saying, Holy, Holy, Holy........

This explains why God, in his nature and likeness, can neither stand iniquity nor behold sin. Nothing impure, defiled, or with any blemish can come near him or survive in his presence. Even the aroma of offerings from the wicked cannot attract God's righteous attention. For such is abomination to him.

> *"The sacrifice of the wicked is an abomination to the LORD: but the prayer of the upright is his delight. The way of the wicked is an abomination unto the LORD: but he loveth him that followeth after righteousness." (Proverbs 5: 8-9).*

The sacrifice of the wicked compares only to the offering of Cain which was presented from his angry soul. And in the intense heat of that anger, he murdered his brother and buried him in a shallow grave. The smoke of every evil sacrifice is demonic in nature and origin, and cannot appease the righteous God.

This is no wonder since the burning flames that radiate around God represent his perfect purity, his flawless holiness, and absolute righteousness. Thus, the flames of this fire constantly honor God as virtuous, declaring that he is the indisputable supernatural being that is morally right.

Spiritual flames have long been interpreted as a symbol of divine presence. And in some instance, God empowers his agents with swords of flaming fire to fulfill his desired purpose. So, apart from announcing the divine presence of God, the spiritual flame can serve as an instrument for divine protection.

"So, he drove out the man; and he placed at the east of the garden of Eden Cherubims, and a flaming sword which turned every way, to keep the way of the tree of life" (Genesis 3:24)

So, from all available data, we can see that there is fire everywhere. Both in heaven, the throne of God, and on earth, his footstool, fire exists in different forms and serves different purposes. In heaven, it ceaselessly declares God's sovereignty, and on the earth, it is God's tool for baptism, divine judgement, and correction.

The fire and smoke that always surround God in heaven give an insight to his mystery, invincibility, greatness, and power. They speak of God's sovereignty and might, not only in heaven, which is his holy habitation, but over the earth and everything he created.

Thus, fire is found everywhere, whether in Heaven or on earth, where it blazes for good or for evil. Fire is there by the east of the garden of Eden as a flaming sword in the hands of the Cherubim.

God stationed the Cherubs with the revolving sword of fire there to guard the path to the tree of life (Genesis 3:24).

After Noah came out of the ark, following the flood destruction that ravaged the ancient and sinful earth of his generation, the first thing he did was set up an altar where he made sacrifice to God. His burn offering on that altar could not be possible without fire. (Genesis 8: 20-21).

Abraham was a friend of God. And he understood that altars were necessary in his walk with God. After he obeyed God and moved from his people as directed by God, he had an encounter where God spoke promises to him. And the next thing he did was to build an altar. This was between Bethel and Ai.

After many years, God spoke to Abraham in a vision reaffirming his earlier promise to reward him. So, as a sign of the commitment to their friendship, God made a covenant with Abraham. During this process, Abraham made offerings of the herd and the flock, including some birds.

Accordingly, he prepared them as God directed him and laid them on the altar. And as the dusk approached, a deep sleep fell upon Abraham, followed by horror of great darkness. And when it was completely dark, a smoking furnace and a burning lamp consumed his sacrifice (Genesis 15: 17-18).

The fire of God's presence was also a tool for to attracting Moses' attention in the wilderness where he was shepherding the flock of his in-law. While this fire burned in the bush, the bush was not consumed. So, Moses stopped to look at that great sight. And because he did, God endorsed him as his mouthpiece to Pharaoh.

Under the influence of the divine fire, Moses' saw his staff turn into a snake. And as he fled from the snake, God told him what to do. And when he did it, the serpent turned again to a staff. In that same mysterious bush fire, holy ground, Moses' hand became leprous in one moment, only to be healed the next.

Also, in the moments prior to Isaiah's call and commission, he caught a rare glimpse of God's glory and majesty in heaven. During those incredibly moments, he saw an innumerable company of angels before the throne of God gloriously praising God for his holiness.

So, in chapter six of Isaiah, the prophet relays the story of that privileged insight into heaven during which session he saw angelic beings worshiping God in solemn praise. In their midst was an altar blazing with coals of fire from where one seraph took a live coal to cleanse Isaiah's lips, purge his sins, and commission him.

Bible figuratively uses fire to describe God's presence. The presence of this fire tells the story of how God guided the children of Israel from Egypt to Canaan. Then, he was a pillar of fire to them by night, and a pillar of cloud, by day. This fire served as their wall of defense and was light to them throughout their journey.

However, there is also the fire which burns in a place known as hell. This squalid place of no return belches with unquenchable fire. It is a place reserved for all unrepentant, wicked people, and all workers of iniquity who chose the transient pleasures of sin in exchange for God's safe and eternal plan for their souls.

These people include those who had no love for others, who showed no kindness or compassion to the needy, and had no empathy for suffering humanity. Anyone who rejected Christ's gift of salvation will also be listed in this category as his name will not be found in the book of life.

> *"And the sea gave up the dead which were in it; and death and hell delivered up the dead which were in them: and they were judged every man according to their works. And death and hell were cast into the lake of fire. This is the second death" (Revelation 20: 13-14).*

The difference between the fire in heaven, which is the fire of God, and the fire which burns in hell, is that hellfire serves only as a tool for eternal punishment for those who rejected God's divine standard on earth. But God uses his holy fire is an instrument of correction. So, he uses it for purposes other than judgement.

The Devil is an expert at putting evil fires to use. His strategy is to steal, to kill, and to destroy. But he starts by gradually eroding a believer's prayer life and fellowship with God. This enables him to pollute that believer's confidence, steal his joy, and trouble his peace, so that he can freely manipulate his soul.

He is a master at pitching humans against God just to separate them from where they can get help. And after he has devastated a soul, he deceives him into blaming God for his errors. And having derailed those gullible souls he abandons them on the public square of self-condemnation, anxiety, and worry.

An anxious person will be depressed and unable to achieve much. Such a condition will make someone commit unnecessary spiritual and emotional errors. And because that soul is confused and stressed out, he will start to isolate himself, begin to hate everything about himself, and condemn everything around him.

This is when people generally lose interest in life, lose their self-esteem, and start to contemplate suicide. And because they have lost touch with the truth, and with divine helpers, they cannot focus on real issues of life that can help them live out their divine purpose.

Remember the young boy in the Bible whose father brought to Jesus to be healed. The boy suffered from terrible seizures for which the Bible referred to him as a lunatic. And because of his condition, he was often thrown into the fire, and at other times into the river.

From ordinary medical consideration, this boy would be diagnosed as an epileptic because of his regular convulsive feats. But his father understood that his son's condition was spiritual, rather than medical. That was why the Devil often threw into the fire to roast him, or into the water, to drown his destiny.

"Lord, have mercy on my son: for he is lunatick, and sore vexed: for ofttimes he falleth into the fire, and oft into the water. And I brought him

> *to thy disciples, and they could not cure him.*
> *Then Jesus answered and said, O faithless and*
> *perverse generation, how long shall I be with you?*
> *how long shall I suffer you? bring him hither to*
> *me. And Jesus rebuked the devil; and he departed*
> *out of him: and the child was cured from that*
> *very hour" (Matthew 17: 15-18)*

A lunatic is a mentally ill person. The root word for the condition is derived from Latin, *luna*, which means "moon". That boy's father understood something about the spiritual circles of the moon and that different "luna" positions can cause intermittent insanity, or lead to mood changes in unstable human minds.

So, his father brought him to Jesus to heal him. And Jesus did so. Not by applying the usual methods used in the lunatic asylum, but by simply quenching the devil's evil fire that was troubling the boy's life. He just cast out the demon of insanity, and this way, publicly disgraced the Devil's own weapon of affliction.

When the fire of God is deposited in a person's life, it will empower him to carryout, not only supernatural things, but to perform difficult physical deeds with ease. That explains why many Bible characters were able to serve God effectively. This fire burned in their lives, and they used it to serve and honor God.

At the heart of the Bible is God's plan to redeem human souls, heal the world, and deliver mankind from bondage to the Devil who wants nothing to do with God. That was why God sent his son, Jesus. And when he came, he gave his life in exchange for the sins of many souls who were in bondage to Satan.

Hard times will be inevitable in life. The enemy will use sickness, disease, and hunger to frustrate believers. But no one should make his life worse by seeking help from foreign god's, cracking under pressure, sulking, or complaining. God expects his children to remain faithful, calm, and wait for their rescue.

Jesus came to earth to free sinful mankind from hardship,

disease, sickness, poverty, and ultimately to remove all suffering. He did this by taking all human sins upon himself and setting the sinners free. This was how he accomplished the redemptive work on the cross by his death, and resurrection.

That is why the Devil is on rampage in these last days that precede the return of Christ for his church. All the terminal sickness, incurable diseases, and poverty are from the kingdom of darkness. They are his tools for punishing those who are living righteously in anticipation of receiving Jesus' promise for abundant life.

The boy that was troubled by the spirit of lunacy used to be thrown into the fire. But his healing, seen in the context of Jesus death and resurrection, points to a future time when no one who is in Christ will suffer the fire of hell. For in the new earth, there will be no more sickness, disease, or suffering.

When Jesus returns for his church, he will establish a new heaven and a new earth devoid of disease, sickness, pain, suffering, or death. There will be no more grief, crying, or mourning because every man's frail, decaying, mortal body, will be changed for a body like that of Jesus' resurrected body. (Revelation 21:1).

In God's original plan for mankind, Suffering was not part of the agenda. It only became part of the world order after the first Adam rebelled against God. But at the return of Christ, the last Adam, there will be no more hardship because of a new heaven and a new earth where the Devil will play no role.

That new earth will overflow with heavenly joy and there will be pleasures for evermore. That is why the Devil is mad at the heirs of salvation who have been designated to inherit the new kingdom with its treasures. And that is the reason he is throwing all manner of things in their way to make them stumble and reject God.

By his new strategy, the Devil is no longer stopping God's children from going to church. Instead, he now goes to church to recruit the believers he can extinguish their fire. This explains why the modern church has so many Christians without Christ, occupying her pews.

The Devil gets very nervous when he encounters a Christian who can pray with fire from his bones. And he is sore worried to see a church that is on fire for God and worshipping in one accord. He fears that kind of place, even though nothing will stop him from trying to destabilize such a congregation.

A church without the fire of God is a dead Church. And a Christian without fire will make himself an easy prey to the Devil. This is why God endowed the church with spiritual power and why "his eyes run to and from the whole earth to show himself strong on behalf of those whose heart is perfect toward him." (2 Chronicles 16: 9).

Spiritual power is a gift from God. It is the means through which the move of God can be experienced in any life or society. It is through friendship with the Holy Spirit that any person can be endowed with this gift. Until a person receives this power, he cannot serve God effectively.

But no matter how powerful the enemy's authority is, it cannot overshadow the influence over a child of God with fire in his bones. So, any Christian can overcome the Devil's temptation by just reminding himself that God, and not the Devil, is the One in control of his life.

And because God always stands behind his faithful children, a Christian should be confident in times of struggles to say to himself, "I can do all things through Christ that strengthens me" (Philippians 4: 13). He can remind himself of God's promise that says, "No weapon fashioned against me shall prosper" (Isaiah 54: 17).

He can stand on the word that says, "Though I walk through the valley of the shadow of death, l shall fear no evil" (Psalm 23: 4). And he can even, like Job the patriarch, say, "Though he slay me, yet will I trust in him: but I will maintain my own ways before him." (Job 13: 15)

Life is full of challenges. But because God is everywhere, he has prepared ways of escape for those who hold on to his promises even when things are not going well. God did not say that his children will have trouble-free lives. And he may not appear to answer all the riddles they pose during times of trials.

But he reassures them that he is with them in every fiery furnace of life. The Devil's trials burn like fire. They are troubling, complicated, and are fashioned to break the backs of God's children. It is the enemy's objective to use all manner of sufferings to turn people away from God.

Yet God is faithful in rewarding all those who persevere in the face of troubles with victory. So, Christians must get smart and refuse to succumb to the pressures of the Devil, their arch enemy. He wants to possess the believer's soul and destroy his destiny (James 5: 10-11).

That is why he must be avoided at all costs. Christians must never forget God's immense love for them for which he sent his son to die for their redemption. He is always present, ever so near, and listens to all his children's prayers. He brings answers to their questions and peace to all areas of their lives.

God demands the believer's unshaken confidence. And this demands that Christians keep their altar of prayer on holy fire, whether in good times or bad times. Every faithful Christian must selflessly and totally submit himself to God and trust that God will work everything out for his good and to His glory.

God wants all mankind to be his friends. This kind of relationship leads to privileges for all those who accept God's hand of fellowship. God desires lifelong commitments with everyone who believes in his heart that Jesus is Lord and who also will confess with his mouth that God raised him up from the dead.

For these Believers, God visits in human form to confide in them, dine with them, speak with them "face to face", and to reveal secrets to them, like he did to Abraham and Moses. And no matter what they go through, he never forsakes them. (Genesis 18:17-18; Exodus 33:11; Deuteronomy 29:29; Isaiah 41:8).

Just being a friend of a righteous person can open great doors of friendship with God, for a person. Ruth's acceptance of Naomi brought her under the cover of God's glory and fire of protection. It also opened the door for her to be the great grandmother of David from whom Jesus descended. (Ruth 1:16-17; Proverbs 18:24).

Loyal Friendship with God is rooted in love. It attracts favors, security, wealth, graces, mercies, and prosperity. And it enshrines a person's name in God's book of life. Friendship with God through the knowledge of Christ gives a person access into the mind of God.

This way, that person gets to know God's will for his life. And by living in obedience to God's word, a Christian will fulfill his divine purpose on earth. The Devil understands all these things. So, his counter strategy is to introduce fiery afflictions and foster resentment in the hearts of believers against God.

By evoking bitterness in the hearts, he provokes Christians to question the wisdom for their faith. However, friendship with God brings a believer's soul into the precincts of his divine, protective glory. And it positions that soul where he can trust him beyond doubt and reap from the abundant riches of his glory.

This is the confidence that helps Christians to deal with all their struggles. It enables them to lean on the faithfulness of God because they trust that he knows what is best for them in all matters of life. So, no matter how intense the fire of the enemy burns, they patiently wait for the deliverer of their souls.

That trust inspired Abraham to deal with his natural fears and handle all the fiery arrows that Satan threw at him during his trying period. It also helped Joseph to withstand the temptations from Potiphar's wife. It was the pillar on which Moses leaned on to confront Pharaoh in Egypt (James 2:23).

It was this friendship with God that enabled people like Moses, David, Daniel, and Ruth, to operate with fiery and audacious faith. At all times, they put their faith in God, "The consuming fire". And because they did, he consumed what was designed by the Devil to consume them.

So, in life, it will be far more important to seek the power of God's spiritual fire than to hunger for earthly power which focuses mainly on the manipulation of human lives, wealth acquisition, and sexual prowess. And like all things in this universe, these things will all pass away someday.

However, the supreme power of God and its fire will remain forever. This supernatural power was Elijah's only credential. It was the authority by which he caused the rain to cease from falling for three and a half years. It was also the power that enabled him to provoke fire and rain from heaven, on his demand.

The same power represented the "fire in prophet Jeremiah's bones". The fire of God generates light. It shines brightly upon the earth, dispersing every satanic darkness. That is why sexual predators, rapists, robbers, and murderers do not like that light. Because it exposes their wicked acts.

The fire of God is a mystery. And while it is everywhere, only God can put it on and only him can put it off. This fire generates glowing light that carries the glory of God to the ends of the earth. And just as the fire of the devil generates a heavy cloud of destruction, the fire of God's presence brings hope and peace.

Supernatural demonstrations of God's power are manifest more frequently where God's holy fire is present. Such fiery expressions of God's divine character open doors of visions, revelation, healings, deliverance, and other outpourings of the Holy Spirit upon man on the earth.

God uses the magnet of his holy fire to attract human attention. And he baptizes men with this intense and passionate fire so they can use its power to serve him. Unfortunately, many people show no concern even when they sight such great and incredible fires. So, this power eludes them.

In this church generation, God is looking for men like Moses who believe in God with their entire being. He is not interested in a congregation like the "church in Philadelphia". It was a pretentious congregation that professed to love God with their mouths, but their hearts were in the club of their master Satan.

Such souls cannot contain the fire of God. It will consume them like it did with the sons of Aaron. God cannot trust gullible people with his supernatural fire. He will not also work through those whose faith is unstable and who lack passion or patience, in their walk with him.

PRAYER POINTS

1) Holy Ghost fire, dry up the root of any tree bearing fruit of generational sickness in my body, in Jesus' name.

2) My body, become too hot for any demon to possess or oppress, in Jesus' name.

3) O God, let the fire of your glory become a blanket and cover my life, in Jesus' name.

4) Demons on assignment to abuse me in my dream, be roasted by fire, in Jesus' name.

5) Fire of God, burn in every area of my body, in Jesus' name.

6) My words, become like fire and consume problems to ashes, in Jesus' name.

7) God of Elijah, disgrace the powers troubling with charm, with your fire, in Jesus' name.

8) Schemes of firebombers designed to roast my life, backfire, in Jesus' name.

9) Fire of God, contend with any evil fire contending with me, in Jesus' name.

10) Dew of heaven, quench the evil fire the enemy is using against my health, in Jesus' name.

11) Fire from the God of Elijah, possess all my battles, in Jesus' name.

12) Holy Ghost fire, destroy everything that is not holy in my life, in Jesus' name.

13) Fire of God, pursue my enemies, find them, and judge them, in Jesus' name.

14) O Lord, release your healing fire from heaven and heal me, in Jesus' name.

CHAPTER 8

THE POWER OF GOD'S FIRE

This world is polluted by sin. As a result, most human achievement is only through hard labor and sweat. Thus, people are under daily stress, afraid of today, unsure of the future, and overwhelmed in their spirit, soul, and body, due to the agony of living life in the misery and mystery of the unknown.

The good news, however, is that the Christian who knows his authority in Christ will not come under these worldly pressures. This is because, by his divine power, God has provided every need required for life and godliness through the knowledge of him who called us by his glory and goodness" (2 Peter 1:3).

But I hasten to add that only those who trust in the Lord, whether in good times or bad times, and are in a relationship with him, can receive those gifts. When a person sincerely surrenders his life to Christ, God gives him the knowledge, wisdom, understanding, and power to outwit life's challenges.

> *"He giveth power to the faint; and to them that*
> *have no might he increaseth strength. Even the*
> *youths shall faint and be weary, and the young*
> *men shall utterly fall: But they that wait upon*
> *the LORD shall renew their strength; they shall*
> *mount up with wings as eagles; they shall run,*

and not be weary; and they shall walk, and not faint (Isaiah 40: 29-31).

One of the reasons God created man is to have a relationship with him. Thus, he sees every one of his human creatures as part of his large family. However, he desires closer family ties with those who believe in his Son. So, through Jesus, God wants all believers to share the closest possible intimate relationship with him.

Everyone in a relationship has a role to play. So, in this relationship with God, every Christian is required to make valuable contributions in areas of faith, love for Christ, and kindness towards others. These are some factors that sustain this relationship and make God's gifts meaningful in the life of his children.

God always listens attentively to the prayers of his children. He hears and answers all their prayers according to his will. He never lets anyone of his children down and does not look the other way when they cry to him while going through a rough time.

But he favors those who relate with him more than the people who do not identify with him. So, the believer's relationship with God should be his number one priority. This relationship demands a life of righteousness. And once a person makes his ways right with God, all things will fall into place in that life.

God endows his faithful friends with power to run for his kingdom without being weary and to walk with him without fainting. But even when they get weak, the unseen hand of God picks them up, leads them to the still waters of life, and refreshes them, so they can continue to walk with him and work for him.

This way, God empowers his children or kindles their lives with fire so they can operate for him in unique ways. His fire distinguishes lives in ways that attract attention wherever they appear. Moses encountered God and was anointed with that fire while he fed the flock of Jethro, his father-in-law, and mentor.

The power of this heavenly anointing burns with such intensity that it changes the trajectory of any destiny that it baptizes. And those who are privileged to be baptized with this fire cannot be ignored. Moses encountered this incredible heavenly fire at Horeb. Thereafter, his life never remained the same.

The life of Moses and the fire of God.

There was a man from the tribe of Levi who married a woman from the tribe of Levi. The woman had a son called Moses. But from the day of this boy's birth, His mother, Jochebed, observed that a special glow upon him and hid him inside the home because it was a time of Egyptian infanticide against Hebrew boys.

For three months, Jochebed hid this unique baby boy. And when she could no longer hide him indoors, she got a little basket made of papyrus, waterproofed it with tar and pitch, placed the child in it, and then she set it afloat by the edge of the river Nile (Exodus 2:1-3).

It was by this edge of the river Nile that grace from heaven spoke to the earth, and God's divine favor caused Pharaoh's daughter to find and rescue this God's future instrument of deliverance. And Pharaoh's daughter named him Moses. Because she said, she drew him out of the water.

So, from babyhood, the mark of God's presence for greatness was already on Moses' life. It was upon his life not just to protect him when he could not protect himself, but to preserve his life till the time of his manifestation was due. When God's fire burns in a person's life, even his mistakes become miracles.

And when the fulness of time came for the manifestation of that fire in Moses' life, it burned with such intensity that, many times, people could not look at him directly in the face because of its glory. So, he often wore a veil to cover his face because of the divine glare that came from his face.

This fire empowered Moses throughout his entire ministry. It emboldened him to go to Pharaoh with messages of deliverance for the children of Israel from God, and prepared him in the process, for communicating with God and receiving the law, which was the constitution of the nation of Israel.

The flame of fire generates light. And in a dark and digital world like ours, people need natural light for sight, and the spiritual light of God that shows the true way. But where there are no believers with the fire of God in them to shine this light, human souls will go in the wrong direction, and many will perish.

Christians are called to be the light in a dark world and not conform to the new cult awakening that is demonizing the universe. It is the fire of God that can show the way to those in the dark, to spread God's good news, heal the sick, set the captives free, break curses, destroy satanic yokes, and terminate evil covenants.

Consider what the same fire did in the life of prophet Elisha. Even his dead body literally carried "burning coals of resurrection fire". The grave could not arrest the power of this fire in his bones. Bible records tell the story of a dead man who was raised to life after he was horridly dumped into Elisha's grave.

Moabite raiders always pillaged the country of Israel during the springtime. But once, while some Israelites were burying a man, they sighted a band of these hoodlums. So, they horridly threw the corpse into a tomb that they did not realize was Elisha's burial place.

And because they were afraid of the Moabite raiders, they fled for safety without concluding the funeral. But the moment the dead body made contact with the bones of Elisha the man came back to life. But realizing he was in a tomb, he jumped out, ran behind those who had earlier come to bury him (2 Kings 13:21).

When this power was in Jeremiah's life, he said it was like fire in his bones. And just like natural blazing fire will keep a person uncomfortable, no one burning with this God's holy fire can have his peace until he speaks that word, either to win souls for God, or to warn sinners of their evil ways.

Evil habits, addictions, compulsive behaviors, and other negative traits and emotions can be reversed, when Christians on fire boldly challenge these works of darkness. Such supernatural works are possible. Because when God's supernatural fire flows through the lives of his natural vessels, it brings positive changes.

God uses his fiery word in the mouth of his chosen vessels to bring comfort, peace, healing, deliverance, or restoration to the world. When a child of God that is invested with his power speaks over any issue, situations change to the glory of God. Such bold, faith-backed actions can shut the heavens or still the storm.

The word of God has power. And it can manifest in the form of burning fire to protect, revive, resurrect, transform, guide, direct, lead, shield, and defend God's interest in his children. Above all, that fire reveals God's gifts in believers and prepares them for service when their talents are needed in God's kingdom.

God makes his ministers fire.

It is not by the accident of creation, but by choice, that when God created angels (spirit beings), he made them his messengers. However, when he formed his ministers, he made them "flames of fire". Thus, God uses all forces of nature and the elements to effectively serve his purposes and intents.

All natural elements, forces, and human agents are God's creatures and are of no less value to God than his angels which are spirits. He formed each of them respectively for some purpose, and whenever he demands, they serve him to his delight. At his command, they move swiftly to do his bidding.

> *"Bless the LORD, O my soul. O LORD my God, thou art very great; thou art clothed with honour and majesty. Who coverest thyself with light as with a garment: who stretchest out the heavens like a curtain: Who layeth the beams of his chambers in the waters: who maketh the clouds his chariot: who walketh upon the wings of the wind: Who*

*maketh his angels spirits; his ministers a flaming
fire:" (Psalm 104: 1-4).*

When God's mark of fire is on a chosen vessel, it endows that individual with power to properly accomplish divine purposes. This helps that person to work in amazing ways and without hinderance, as God's angels do. This incredible privilege makes a person bold, active, and very fit for his assignment.

When divine fire is upon God's human agents, they are as powerful as his angels (who are spirit beings). That explains why natural men like Moses, Elijah, Elisha, and Jesus Christ, could control the winds, the tempest, the storms, and the rain, through the word of faith they spoke.

*"And he arose, and rebuked the wind, and said
unto the sea, Peace, be still. And the wind ceased,
and there was a great calm" (Mark 4:39).*

When Jesus spoke to the storm that threatened to sink the boat, as he sailed with his disciples, it immediately became calm. This is the portion of all children of God who know their right in Christ. And the whole creation is waiting for the manifestation of such believers.

Also, the supernatural God is waiting to deploy those Christians who are ready to manage the elements, the clouds, the body of waters, and all God's workmanship on earth, for him. But he will only use fire-baptized Christians, as the tools to accomplish his supernatural feats.

The rage of the Devil.

The Devil understands that God's agenda for mankind is to use overcomers to repopulate and repossess the new earth. So, he is doing everything he can to drag as many people as possible to hell and deny them that great purpose of God. And he is using every evil design to accomplish his own plan.

That is why every Christian must be sure of the fire burning on the altar of his soul. Today, false doctrines have been injected into the Bible and are been preach from church pulpits as the truth. But a judgement day will come when all believers shall account for what they allowed into the secret places of their hearts.

The fires of lust, evil sexual appetite, demonic sensual imagination, rape, and pornography are destructive embers that the Devil is fanning into flames in the minds of people. Christians must therefore be careful because the Devil delights in seductively wooing people to his side before destroying them.

He is a rule- breaker and restless busy-body. He does not sleep a wink, but is always moving up and down, roaming about the earth, searching for whom he may destroy. He specializes in generating problems and in making life miserable for God's children.

"Now there was a day when the sons of God came to present themselves before the LORD, and Satan came also among them. And the LORD said unto Satan, Whence comest thou? Then Satan answered the LORD, and said, From going to and fro in the earth, and from walking up and down in it. And the LORD said unto Satan, Hast thou considered my servant Job, that there is none like him in the earth, a perfect and an upright man, one that feareth God, and escheweth evil? Then Satan answered the LORD, and said, Doth Job fear God for nought? Hast not thou made an hedge about him, and about his house, and about all that he hath on every side? thou hast blessed the work of his hands, and his substance is increased in the land. But put forth thine hand

now, and touch all that he hath, and he will curse thee to thy face" (Job 1: 6-11).

"And the LORD said unto Satan, Hast thou considered my servant Job, that there is none like him in the earth, a perfect and an upright man, one that feareth God, and escheweth evil? and still he holdeth fast his integrity, although thou movedst me against him, to destroy him without cause. And Satan answered the LORD, and said, Skin for skin, yea, all that a man hath will he give for his life. But put forth thine hand now, and touch his bone and his flesh, and he will curse thee to thy face. And the LORD said unto Satan, Behold, he is in thine hand; but save his life. So went Satan forth from the presence of the LORD, and smote Job with sore boils from the sole of his *(Job 2:3-7).*

The Devil never rests until he accomplishes an evil purpose. He followed his agenda against the patriarch Job till he reduced everything he possessed to ruins. But unbeknown to him, God was with Job. In the same manner, Satan planned against Jesus until he had this righteous man crucified on the cross.

Thus, while believers can trust the ceaseless burning fire of God, which works for their benefit, they must be vigilant and be on the alert because the Devil strikes without warning. That is why no one must engage in spiritual warfare without first probing the reason for his challenge.

So, when a fiery battle arises in a person's life, that person should pause and ask himself questions about what may have provoked the challenge before going into battle. And even during the process of warfare, Christians should not rely on their physical strength, but on the word of "Jehovah, the Man of war".

The expression of the believer's unshaken confidence in God puts heaven on red alert when a child of God is in trouble. This invites God into the picture. And when he gets involved, he comes in the brightness of his glory to gird that believer with strength for the battle or to rescue him from the problem he is facing.

> *"I have pursued mine enemies, and overtaken them: neither did I turn again till they were consumed. I have wounded them that they were not able to rise: they are fallen under my feet. For thou hast girded me with strength unto the battle: thou hast subdued under me those that rose up against me" (Psalm 18: 37-39)*

From the moment a person is born again, he becomes an enemy of the Devil by default. As a result, demons set him up as an instant target for evil darts by day and arrows of pestilence in the dark. So, such a person must never entertain any divided loyalty. All his devotion must be to please God and God alone.

This is because the enemy will set up that person for scrutiny from then on, whether in public or private. And any mistake he makes will be used against him in the satanic court where he can easily be indicted, because there, the enemy is the judge, prosecutor, and jury there.

Believers must therefore hunger to be filled with the gifts of the Holy Spirit and be baptized by God's holy fire. These will help Christians to overcome the enemy's revamped evil schemes. He is using every deadly weapon in his arsenal on this assault to destroy the children of God.

Perversity is a regular item on his menu, deceit is his first course, violence is his main dish, and drugs constitute his best deserts. He has also repackaged himself to attract Christians through a series of finely coordinated occult activities and witchcraft worship that easily seduce the human mind.

On a regular basis, he now uses evil fire from the dark world to attack church growth in places like China, Africa, East, and Western Europe, and in the Middle East. More than ever before, the church, Christians, and Christianity are facing threats of annihilation by the fire from the dark world.

Everyone is fair game; young, old, male, female, Black, Brown, or White. No one is exempt from the ruthless threats and painful challenges. And where systematic torture, genocide, persecution, and hunger, do not work fast for him, he engages the services of false prophets and Pentecostal witches.

Right now, the enemy's strategy is to torment human souls. He believes that by making the world sick, he can provoke Christians to deny God's sovereignty and lordship. A closer look at what is going on in our world today will reveal the damage the devil has done and is still doing.

One thing the Devil does very well is to market himself as a harmless angel of light. This way, he can easily attract his victims and take them captive. Before they realize it, they become his slaves here on earth. And in the end, he will take them to hell to make them his eternal slaves.

That is why he is busy inspiring demonic but seductive music, immoral fashion designs, perverse street language, evil sexual styles, and deadly alcohol and drug habits from the pit of hell. Many people are already hooked on these evil appetites. But they do not know that the end of it is hellfire.

Like in the days on Noah, people are comfortably carousing in evil lifestyles today while Satan is busy tattooing sin on their minds via the internet, cell phones, digital platforms, and other media, all of which are the fast routes to human hearts whose gates are not guarded by God's angels with their swords of fire.

The reason that Satan seduces human minds is to take their attention away from God and focus them on material things that will not help those souls prepare for eternity in heaven. The good news however is that no matter how far away on the wrong road a person has traveled, he can still make a U-turn and return to God.

It was for this reason that God himself came to be part of this hostile world, in human form, as Jesus, to save it. So, the Devil loves to trip Christians, to cause to fall and break into many pieces. So, every believer must be determined not to stay down. Instead, learn to look up to God who can remold his destiny.

There is power in God's fire to melt human broken pieces and remold that person again. When a person baptized by the fire of God speaks, things happen in the spirit realm and even the earth cooperates with his injunctions, decrees, and commands. Satan fears such people.

The prayers of such children of God invoke supernatural activities that force the earth to comply with their desires irrespective of the conditions of nature. Their words of prophecy suspend natural laws and cause things in their environment to be rearranged in their favor.

Word of prophecy from a believer that is baptized by fire will lead to healing of sicknesses, cause deliverance, save generations from bloodline bondage, and bring God's people out from their oppression. Miracles, restorations, and open doors can only be possible when God's children on fire stand up against the Devil.

Ancestral evil abominations may hold a community in captivity. But just one command by a righteous child of God has the power to nullify all long-standing curses, break evil soul ties, counter satanic oaths, and destroy evil yokes. That is why God is looking for men he will baptize with the fire to operate in this power.

Before the fire of God was kindled in the life of Gideon, the giant in his destiny had been in a state of satanic comatose. So, this Gideon continued to live in fearful timidity and in spiritual impotence until he had an encounter with an angel of the Lord that helped him recalibrate his perception of himself.

From then on, the same Gideon who hitherto had lived in mortal fear of his enemies and had shown no concern for the evil altar of Baal in his father's house, could no longer resist the burning urge to pull down that evil altar sustaining his problems. And when he did, he reclaimed his destiny and community for God.

The power in God's fire empowers a Christian with the boldness to turn and pursue his pursuers. It awakens his ears, moment by moment, to hear what God is saying, opens his eyes to see opportunities that others cannot perceive, and makes his feet to quickly follow the path where God is leading him.

This holy fire clearly reveals a person's purpose to him, making him bolder, stronger, wiser, and more understanding of the various dimensions of what God has called them to do with his life. It also helps a person to stand strong through the storms of the ministry and stay strong against the enemy's attacks.

PRAYER POINTS

1) Holy Spirit, turn my words into fire and use them to change lives for the kingdom, in Jesus' name.

2) Blood of Jesus, render null and void the Witchcraft judgement over my life, in Jesus' name.

3) By the authority of Jesus' cross, I terminate every curse I put on my head, in Jesus' name.

4) Fire of God, dry up any genetic ailment troubling my life, in Jesus' name.

5) Fire of God, consume the powers calling my name for evil, in Jesus' name.

6) Altars of darkness feeding on my destiny, collapse by fire, in Jesus' name.

7) Holy Ghost fire make my body a hostile environment for any sickness, in Jesus' name.

8) Fire of God, make my body too hot to accommodate cancer, in Jesus' name.

9) By the promise of God's word, no fire shall consume me, in Jesus' name.

10) Divine arrows of fire, pursue and destroy my stubborn attackers, in Jesus' name.

11) I pull down every evil altar working against my potentials, in Jesus' name.

12) God that answers by fire, step into my difficult situations, in Jesus' name.

13) Powers challenging my destiny from the altar of darkness, be roasted by fire, in Jesus' name.

14) O God, disappoint anyone mocking me for trusting you, in Jesus' name.

CHAPTER 9

THE GOD OF ELIJAH

In the Bible, many individuals were associated with the character of fire because it operated in their lives in ways more than it did in others. The fire of God burned immensely in those lives and impacted their ministries positively. Among such characters were very ordinary people like Hananiah, Mishel, and Azariah.

These characters were outstanding children of God, anointed with the incredible power of God's fire. Elijah, the Tishbite, was also one such person. This child of God turned out to be a very spectacular "fiery" voice in Israel, in ways that none of his peers did, during a turbulent time in the history of that nation.

When prophets spoke the word of God in the Bible era, things happened. But Elijah operated even on a higher dimension in his application of God's word. For this reason, many Christians still pray today invoking the manifestation of the "God of Elijah", who goes by the title, "the God that answers by fire".

The name Elijah in the Greek language is Elias. In Old Testament Hebrew text, it literally means "Jehovah is God". But this Elijah was neither Jehovah nor God but just an ordinary human being with audacious faith who God used in very unexplainable ways, during a time of godlessness in Israel.

Judaism began as a monotheist religion that Abraham founded after God revealed himself to him as the only Sovereign God. But by the time King Ahab and his wife ruled Israel, the nation of Israel, who were descendants of Abraham, had embraced Canaanite gods and shamelessly slipped into idol worship.

The works and prayer-life of Elijah

Prophet Elijah was a man greatly anointed by God. The extraordinary glory of God's presence was much upon him that it set his ministry apart. Whenever he spoke as a mouth piece of God, things happened exactly as he desired them to be. And his mere presence caused things to fall into their natural places.

He was a treasured weapon of war in God's hand, a natural man whose voice literally invoked flaming fire, and a superhero that achieved great stature with God. On this account, God fed him supernaturally, sustained him in uncommon ways during uncommon times, protected him from his enemies, and used him mightily.

Elijah was a Jew, but he was of the stock that feared God and respected his law. So, the Sovereign God used him supremely in the outstanding defense of his commandments. As a result, his ministry was so emblematic of fire that other great prophets, like Elisha, prayed in the name of "the Lord God of Elijah".

Prophet Elijah was undoubtedly a man sent by God. He was an ordinary man made extraordinary by the powerful word of God, and the way he handled it. He was a hairy man and always wore a leather belt around his waist. This prophet was a spiritual colossus with National clout.

And he showed great concern for fundamental issues that threatened God's law, matters that affected the nation, and had the courage to bring the hearts of all Israel back to God. And when he spoke, the earth obeyed, the elements took notice, and the heavens respected his order.

In ancient Israel, the sacred Judaic worship of One God, the

Almighty, living and Sovereign God, of Abraham, Isaac, and Jacob, was the only acceptable model. But many times, godless Kings and leaders in Israel defied this model of worship and introduced foreign gods from heathen nations.

Elijah lived and ministered during and beyond the reign of King Ahab and his idolatrous wife. These two walked in the sinful ways of earlier Kings of Israel. King Ahab and his wife Jezebel celebrated Baal, the god of the Sidonians, with shameless boldness and dragged the nation of Israel into a state of godlessness.

In ancient Canaanite society, Baal was a deity ascribed with power to cause dew and rain. He was worshipped as the god of fertility and often offered ritualistic sacrifices which included burning children alive on altars erected to his name. And amid horrific screams of dying children, the worshippers engaged in sexual orgies.

Jezebel was a Sidonian princess who married Ahab after this King of Israel went into alliance with the King of Sidon. So, it was easy for Jezebel to seduce the King and cause him to turn the spiritual eyes of the nation of Israel away from the Sovereign God, the God of Abraham.

In the divided Kingdom of Israel, the Northern block was known for their unfaithfulness as their Kings often flirted with foreign gods. They rejected their covenant with God, tore down his altars, put his prophets to death, and built evil altars in high places and under the groves, to deify idols.

> *"And he said, I have been very jealous for the*
> *LORD God of hosts: because the children of Israel*
> *have forsaken thy covenant, thrown down thine*
> *altars, and slain thy prophets with the sword;*
> *and I, even I only, am left; and they seek my life,*
> *to take it away." (1 Kings 19: 14).*

As a result of the apostasy of the Northern Kingdom, the priesthood became corrupt. This motivated the remaining faithful

Prophets, Priests, and Levites, to move over to the southern Kingdom of Judah. These priests and Levites remained in Jerusalem from where they ministered in the temple.

Baal was an ancient deity generally worshipped by the Canaanites. So, the practice of Baal worship was vehemently condemned in God's law to Moses for all Israel. Yet in the stubbornness of their hearts, the children of Israel often embraced foreign deities. And such acts always brought the wrath of God's fire upon them.

Long before the period of the Judges in Israel, the attraction to idol worship always existed among the children of Israel. This romance prompted the setting up of the Golden Calf, which Aaron made for them to worship during their wilderness journey to Canaan. Following this evil action, many Israelites lost their lives.

> *"And he received them at their hand, and fashioned it with a graving tool, after he had made it a molten calf: and they said, These be thy gods, O Israel, which brought thee up out of the land of Egypt. And when Aaron saw it, he built an altar before it; and Aaron made proclamation, and said, Tomorrow is a feast to the LORD. And they rose up early on the morrow, and offered burnt offerings, and brought peace offerings; and the people sat down to eat and to drink and rose up to play. And the LORD said unto Moses, Go, get thee down; for thy people, which thou broughtest out of the land of Egypt, have corrupted themselves:" (Exodus 32: 4-7).*

And in a move that seemed to replicate this ugly history, King Jeroboam made two golden calves during his reign. He placed one calf at Bethel in the south and the other at Dan in the north. He believed this would kill people's desire from going to worship in temple in Jerusalem; a move that would weaken his kingdom.

This Jeroboam was a godless, idol loving King known for consecrating his own priests. During his time, he abolished the worship of the true God of Abraham and established the worship of dead Canaanite idols following the pattern of Aaron who built a Golden calf for the children of Israel during their wilderness journey.

The Golden calf at Bethel was indeed a direct afront to Abraham's first altar there, where he worshipped God. So, King Jeroboam's golden calf was a supreme ridicule to the altar Abraham originally raised at Bethel. This was Jeroboam's way of elevating a mere idol to the level to which the Sovereign God was reverenced.

King Jeroboam's absurd act of apostasy was not only a rejection of faith in the sovereign, true, and living God, but was also designed to divert the heart of God's children from worshiping God. And as penalty for these heinous acts, God destroyed his dynasty.

> *"Then Jeroboam built Shechem in mount Ephraim, and dwelt therein; and went out from thence, and built Penuel. And Jeroboam said in his heart, Now shall the kingdom return to the house of David: If this people go up to do sacrifice in the house of the LORD at Jerusalem, then shall the heart of this people turn again unto their lord, even unto Rehoboam king of Judah, and they shall kill me, and go again to Rehoboam king of Judah. Whereupon the king took counsel, and made two calves of gold, and said unto them, It is too much for you to go up to Jerusalem: behold thy gods, O Israel, which brought thee up out of the land of Egypt. And he set the one in Bethel, and the other put he in Dan. And this thing became a sin: for the people went to worship before the one, even unto Dan."*
> *(1 Kings 12: 25-30)*

Before kings ruled in Israel, Judges were in-charge of nation. But these Judges most often led God's children astray. For this reason, the people always faced God's wrath. Whenever they broke God's laws, he permitted their enemy's armies to defeat them in battles and to carry them into captivity.

This continued through the reign of King Ahab. This very infamous King Ahab was the son of Omri. He was one, in a chain of many evil kings of the nation (northern kingdom) of Israel who had fallen in love with the idolatrous teachings of their generation.

In their days, they chose the evil religious paths of their Canaanite neighbors over the godly teachings of Judaism and the exclusive worship of the Hebrew God of Abraham. Thus, it was easy for Ahab, after he became king and got married to Jezebel, to buckle under the evil influence of his Sidonian neighbors' and in-laws.

Jezebel was the daughter of the Priestly-King, Ethbaal, who ruled the ungodly nation of Sidon (in the present-day Lebanon). Her marriage to Ahab was equivalent to bringing evil fire into God's holy temple, as it led him to completely lose his faith and drag the Northern Kingdom of Israel into vicious abomination.

But this was during the time of Elijah. So, this fearless prophet boldly spoke out for God against the despicable ways of the King. As a result, there was no one hated more in the land of Israel by King Ahab and Queen Jezebel than Prophet Elijah. This put his life in jeopardy.

Elijah saw that the evil in the royal court violated God's law and defiled the temple worship. So, he forthrightly pointed out the sin to the King and condemned it. This made his ministry a literal fishbone in the throat of the ungodly King who labelled him the "troubler of Israel".

"And it came to pass, when Ahab saw Elijah, that Ahab said unto him, Art thou he that troubleth Israel?" (1 Kings 18: 17).

Prophet Elijah began his ministry as a bold pillar of faith. He was a man who trusted very much in the supernatural power of God's word. And he relied on this great power of God's word to perform many outstanding miracles and to defeat the enemies of God such as King Ahab.

The King was a very rebellious ruler who went against God's directives. He disobeyed God's command to destroy Ben-hadad. God had led Israel to victory over Syria and directed that King Ahab destroy Ben-hadad. Instead, Ahab made a treaty with Ben-hadad, the King of Syria who he was supposed to destroy (1 Kings 20).

But the final nail that sealed King Ahab's coffin was his foray into Naboth's vineyard. King Ahab coveted Naboth's vineyard and offered to buy it. But Naboth refused to sell or exchange it for another vineyard because it was his inheritance, and the Law forbade him to sell it (1 Kings 21: 2-3; Leviticus 25: 23).

But Jezebel arranged the murder of Naboth to enable the King to possess the poor man's vineyard for himself.

After this incident, Elijah came to Ahab and gave him an eerie message. He told him that the Lord would cut off all his descendants. And that the King will suffer a disgraceful death, with dogs licking his blood in the same way they licked the blood of Naboth. (1 Kings 21:19).

Prophet Elijah's prophecy against Ahab came true exactly as he predicted. Ahab's own false prophets enticed him into battle at Ramoth-Gilead where he was hit by a "random" arrow, and he slowly bled to death in his chariot. Ahab perished, burned by the fire he carried on his lap. He married an idolatrous wife.

And later, as they washed his chariot at a pool in Samaria, dogs came and licked up his blood, as the word of the man of God said. Also, after Ahab's death, Jehu orchestrated the murder of his wife Jezebel and everyone else of the descendants of King Ahab (1 Kings 22: 38; 2 Kings 9; 2 Kings 10).

However, despite the brazen acts of fire in the life of Elijah, he succumbed to the emotions of fear. At one point in his life, he fled from the people who should be running away from him. Yet, notwithstanding this display of human frailty, the prophet never lost God's favor.

During the time of his misery, he ran into a cave to hide from his adversaries and pleaded with God to take his life. Yet in all his afflictions, God continued to protect and provide for him in uncommon ways. Once, God used the services of ravens to serve him lunch, and another time, he used a widow to care for him.

ELIJAH'S MINISTRY AND MIRACLES.

Elijah was a man with unique human virtues and incomparable spiritual characteristics. It is true he was an ordinary, natural man. But his consecrated dedication to God, firm commitment to duty, boldness before kings and men, and fearlessness before false prophets, surpass that of most of his contemporaries.

His ministry was associated with astounding miracles that amazed lovers of righteous signs and wonders, even though it attracted threats for him from the enemies of God. His methods were unusual, and his approaches were dramatic. But they produced outstanding results.

Prophet Elijah was very defensive of God's laws and fearlessly condemned idolatry and its patrons. For these reasons, God rewarded him with the uncommon experience of passing from life to glory without dying like all men. And even after he was translated to heaven, he continued to do missionary work on earth.

"And after six days Jesus taketh with him Peter, and James, and John, and leadeth them up into an high mountain apart by themselves: and he was transfigured before them. And his raiment became shining, exceeding white as snow; so as no fuller on earth can white them. And there appeared unto them Elias with Moses: and they were talking with Jesus. And Peter answered and said to Jesus, Master, it is good for us to be here: and let us make three tabernacles; one for thee, and one for Moses, and one for Elias. For he wist not what to say; for they were sore afraid. And there was a cloud that overshadowed them: and a voice came out of the cloud, saying, This is my beloved Son: hear him. And suddenly, when they had looked round about, they saw no man any more, save Jesus only with themselves." (Mark 9: 2-8).

This powerful prophet, according to Bible records, was visibly present, on the day of Christ's transfiguration. This significant event in the life of Jesus was a proof of his divinity. And while it was to strengthen him for his crucifixion it also confirms that Jesus is the connecting point between man and God.

The inerrant word of God, according to apostle Mark, confirms that prophet Elijah was present during the transfiguration of Christ. God is very delighted with "men on fire" like Elijah, Moses, Daniel, Noah, Job, and others. And he never ceases to boast about their righteousness.

"And after six days Jesus taketh with him Peter, and James, and John, and leadeth them up into an high mountain apart by themselves: and he was transfigured before them. And his raiment became shining, exceeding white as snow; so as no fuller on earth can white them. And there appeared unto them Elias with Moses: and they were talking with Jesus. And Peter answered and said to Jesus, Master, it is good for us to be here: and let us make three tabernacles; one for thee, and one for Moses, and one for Elias" (Mark 9: 2-5).

He uniquely represented and glorified the Sovereign God in ways that made King Ahab and Jezebel to fear him, showing that he was indeed a mighty prophet of God. The story of this selfless, and courageous servant of God will be incomplete without recapturing some of the uncommon miracles he performed.

He was zealous for the true God and single handedly challenged the many false prophets in Israel. But while he was bold in his several confrontations against King Ahab and Jezebel, the personal struggles he had during the dwindling days of his ministry exposed his humanity.

Sometimes, servants of God get into trouble too. Abraham was in distress, Jeremiah was discouraged, Jesus was tempted and felt forsaken, Joseph feared he was abandoned, and John the Baptist felt frustrated. At some point, Elijah was overcome by loneliness, became afraid of Jezebel, and fled into the wilderness.

Still, in those weary conditions, the God of grace who called them to his eternal glory never abandoned them. He was always there every step of the way, strengthening, catering, and comforting them. And he never failed to meet them at the very points of their spiritual and basic needs (1 Peter 5: 10).

Whenever bad things happen to the righteous, God comes to their rescue. If he does not snatch them away from the problem, he gives them strength to battle through those situations. He watches over them as a bodyguard and protects them, shielding every bone in their bodies so that not one gets broken (Psalms 34:19-20).

During the time of Elijah, the godless Canaanites believed that the Baal had power to cause rain and give dew. His titles were, "Lord of the Heavens" and "the storm god who rides on the clouds". So, this god, whose symbol was represented by a bull, was highly venerated. And Israel copied them under Ahab and Jezebel.

But Elijah's appearance on the scene, and the manner he disproved this false claim before all Israel, was unprecedented. His display was a great blow against the long-celebrated myth conceived by the godless Sidonians and shared by the nation of Israel who by then had wandered away from what was right before God.

ELIJAH AND THE PROPHETS OF BAAL.

In ancient Canaanite mythology, Baal had several titles depending on the nation that worshiped him. Apart from "the lord of Rain and Dew", he was called "the prince or storm god" who rides on the clouds, in one place, and in another, he was known as "lord of the heavens".

By Canaanite beliefs, fertility was perceived to operate in seven-year cycles, controlled by Baal, the god of life. Baal was said to be in mortal battle against another Canaanite deity known as "Mot", the god of death and sterility. The two were constantly contesting for control of each successive seven-year cycle.

The idea was that the one who triumphed over the other took control of that seven-year cycle. If Baal was the victor, he ruled over that seven-year cycle of fertility. But if "Mot" prevailed, he presided over a period of sterility, drought, famine, and death.

King Ahab, his godless wife Jezebel, and all Israel had become part of this despicable Baal worship in defiance to God's law. God had distinguished Israel from other nations to be his very own. Sadly, under most kings of Israel, the nation prostituted herself in rituals to the god Molech contrary to divine laws and statutes (Leviticus 20:1-6).

But King Ahab and his wife Jezebel took these evil practices and beliefs to a much higher dimension. And because the King championed unholy living, the people followed suit. So, the whole nation was in rebellion against Jehovah and burned evil incense (evil fires) to strange gods.

Those who did not fear God followed the idolatrous ways of King Ahab and his wife Jezebel. They continued in their horrible idolatry, freely enjoying the lewd privileges it offered them. The demonic spirit behind Jezebel was powerful, and it enabled her to control everyone in Israel including the King.

Jezebel was a proud, arrogant, and unrepentant soul, whose lying spirit never let her submit to godly authority. She operated by a high-level witchcraft spirit that was all about manipulation. And her goal was to destroy the lives of God's children through ungodly sex and other perverse ways.

The Jezebel spirit was a powerful demonic spirit that operated freely in Israel during the time of King Ahab and Jezebel. So, the witchcraft desecration of the land continued unabated until a man of God with holy anger against the disrespect for God's laws and statutes arose in Israel.

This man was Elijah. One day, he went to the King and announced that God was about to bring a judgment of wrath on the kingdom of Israel. One would think that this scary message would move King Ahab and his wife Jezebel to repent for their sins. But it did not.

Rather, they continued to believe in the prophecies of their false prophets. They trusted that the words of the prophets of Baal and Asherah would counter the word of God spoken by a true prophet in the class of Elijah. But the words of this fiery prophet of God put them to shame.

There were four hundred prophets of Baal and four hundred and fifty prophets of Asherah that ate at the table of Jezebel, in the royal court. They made the people believe that it was in Baal's power to cause rain or withhold dew, the two elements that were necessary for good harvest.

These false prophets convinced the people to believe that the god, Baal controlled, not only the womb of the skies, but the womb of the earth, and the womb of the woman. And because the worship of Baal permitted indiscriminate bisexual orgies, the people of Israel loved it.

King Ahab and Jezebel continued to lead the entire nation to believe this falsehood, until God sent Elijah to prove to them that only the Sovereign God has power over the heavens, the earth, fertility, life, and death. Thus, Prophet Elijah went to the royal palace of Israel and drew the battle line.

> *"And Elijah the Tishbite, who was of the inhabitants of Gilead, said unto Ahab, As the LORD God of Israel liveth, before whom I stand, there shall not be dew nor rain these years, but according to my word" (1Kings 17: 1).*

From Bible records, we find that each time God's children rejected his law and commandments, he turned his back on them. And many of those times, they suffered the consequences of their sordid actions. On this occasion, the punishment was a long period of drought and famine.

Sadly, when such things happen, both the righteous and the unrighteous are affected. So, for these three and half years when there was neither dew nor rain in the land of Israel, according to the word of prophet Elijah, even animals suffered the hardship.

> *"My people are destroyed for lack of knowledge: because thou hast rejected knowledge, I will also reject thee, that thou shalt be no priest to me: seeing thou hast forgotten the law of thy God, I will also forget thy children." (Hosea 4: 6).*

> *"Therefore, my people are gone into captivity, because they have no knowledge: and their honourable men are famished, and their multitude dried up with thirst." (Isaiah 5: 13).*

Throughout history, we read that Israel's Northern Kingdom had no faithful kings. Their Kings had an insatiable lust for foreign gods. And in their unfaithfulness, they led the people into serious problems that attracted the wrath of the sovereign God of their father, Abraham.

Most of the Northern Kings of Israel were morally corrupt and spiritually inept. And to satisfy their godless appetites, they often appointed priests who served their personal interests rather than the purpose of God. Under such kings, the few honest Priests and Levites that remained in the land, migrated to Judah.

King Ahab was one of the worst kings of Israel. He was very evil in the sight of the Lord and was married to Jezebel. This Jezebel was the daughter of Eth-Baal, the king of the Phoenician city-state of Tyre. At the height of their reign, they had eight hundred and fifty prophets of Baal and Asherah that ate at their table.

In the New Testament Bible, Jesus rebuked the church in Thyatira for tolerating the Jezebel spirit. However, way back in the Old Testament era, one fearless prophet called Elijah understood never to tolerate, but to confront the wicked, shameless, impudent, and idolatrous woman, called Jezebel.

"Notwithstanding I have a few things against thee, because thou sufferest that woman Jezebel, which calleth herself a prophetess, to teach and to seduce my servants to commit fornication, and to eat things sacrificed unto idols" (Revelation 2: 20).

But under the watch of godless rulers like King Ahab and his wife Jezebel, Israel became a land desecrated by blood through the gruesome sacrifice of babies and burning of incense to foreign gods. This despicable act practiced by heathen nations, was something God had warned the children of Israel against.

And because there were no God-fearing people to present the true word of God and his law to the people in an uncompromising manner, Israel descended into spiritual and moral decay. In times like that, God always sought for fire-baptized believers to rescue his people.

Elijah was one of the first in the line of uncompromising prophets who God sent to Israel and Judah. And when Prophet Elijah confronted King Ahab, he told him in very clear and unmistaken terms that there would be no rain nor dew for some years. This was going to be the penalty for Ahab's and Jezebel's misdeeds.

"And Elijah the Tishbite, who was of the inhabitants of Gilead, said unto Ahab, As the LORD God of Israel liveth, before whom I stand, there shall not be dew nor rain these years, but according to my word." (1 Kings 17: 1).

Those who worshipped Baal believed that he was the god who gave the rains responsible for bountiful harvests. So, the King was sorely distraught when this man of God, Prophet Elijah, boldly asserted in his presence, "that there will be no rain nor dew" for a couple of years.

This bold confrontation proved to King Ahab and Queen Jezebel that the power to bring the dew or cause rainfall was not with Baal or any man. He showed them that this power resided only with the Sovereign God, the creator of the entire universe and all things in it.

By this simple but uncommon decree, Prophet Elijah sealed the heavens over the land of Israel. This way, he proved that there was a power far greater than the power of any heathen god. As a result, there was no rain nor dew for three and a half years, because of Elijah's command.

WIDOW OF ZAREPHATH.

Immediately after this feat, God led Elijah to the brook Cherith, which was by the Jordan. And for many days and nights, God protected, provided, and cared for him there. He instructed ravens to send daily rations of bread and flesh to him, for breakfast and dinner, while he drank water from the brook.

But after the brook dried up, God commanded Elijah to proceed to the house of a poor widow in Zarephath. This was a Phoenician city at the time, but God sent Elijah to embark on a forty day's journey, because he needed him to miraculously save lives in that foreign land too.

Before Elijah encountered this widow, she only had one last meal left in her house. And at the gate of the city where they met, this widow was gathering sticks to make that last handful of meal for herself and her only son. This was supposed to be their final meal before surrendering to death by famine.

But at the request of this strange man, the widow prepared the cake in faith and set it before Elijah to eat first. She gave him water too. And because she did according to the word of God by the mouth of his prophet, this widow, her son, and her household, never lacked food for the rest of that famine season.

> *"And Elijah said unto her, Fear not; go and do as thou hast said: but make me thereof a little cake first, and bring it unto me, and after make for thee and for thy son. For thus saith the LORD God of Israel, The barrel of meal shall not waste, neither shall the cruse of oil fail, until the day that the LORD sendeth rain upon the earth. And she went and did according to the saying of Elijah: and she, and he, and her house, did eat many days. And the barrel of meal wasted not, neither did the cruse of oil fail, according to the word of the LORD, which he spake by Elijah."*
> *(1 Kings 17: 13--16).*

Now, one day, while Elijah was still living in the home of this widow, the only son of this widow became ill. And because the sickness was painful and severe, the boy died suddenly. The woman became very distraught, fearing that the presence of the prophet in her house had brought her sin to light.

But Elijah took the dead body of the lad from her mother and carried him up to his own bed on the attic. And while in that place, he cried to God and stretched himself upon the body of the child, three times. And following Elijah's prayer, the dead boy was revived. (1 Kings 17: 17-22).

Elijah was an unusual type of prophet and his extraordinary miracles set him apart from other prophets of his time. He was an ordinary human, but in matters of faith, his ministry literally operated on "spiritual steroids". He had fiery zeal for God and his methods were very dramatic.

He did not fear any King no matter how uncomfortable the message from God was to them. And he was never scared of the cultic antics of false prophets that served the king. Even their number never troubled him. He was certain that one with God was in the majority and he showed this on Mount Carmel.

THE BATTLE ON MOUNT CARMEL.

After three and half years of intense drought and harsh famine in the land of Israel, which Elijah commanded, he reappeared again on the scene. At the mandate of God, he was directed to show himself to King Ahab before God could send rain upon the land of Israel.

In the years during which Elijah locked the heavens above Ahab's kingdom and walked away with the key literally in his pocket, the prophets of Baal had no answer to the problem of drought. So, Elijah went to show himself to King Ahab, in obedience to the word of God.

"And it came to pass after many days, that the word of the LORD came to Elijah in the third year, saying, Go, shew thyself unto Ahab; and I will send rain upon the earth. And Elijah went to shew himself unto Ahab. And there was a sore famine in Samaria." (1 Kings 18: 1-2).

During those days of drought and famine, life became so unbearable as there was no water to drink or fodder to sustain the horses and mules. Thus, there was serious concern that they could lose all the remaining beasts. So, the King sent out his servant Obadiah to search wherever he could find water in all the land.

While the King went one way in search of water and grass to save the beasts,

Obadiah went another direction. But as Obadiah went on his way, he met Prophet Elijah. And even though he recognized him, he wanted to be sure he was not in a trance. So, he asked him, "Art thou that my lord, Elijah?"

Obadiah was one of the few faithful servants of God who remained in the service of King Ahab through this godless period. And while Jezebel embarked on eliminating God's prophets from the land of Israel, Obadiah had hidden a hundred of them in caves and fed them daily with bread and water.

Obadiah knew how much King Ahab wanted to arrest Prophet Elijah. So, he feared that the King would kill him if he reported he had seen Prophet Elijah and let him slip away. However, prophet Elijah allayed his fears and assured him that he would make himself available, and he did.

Thus, through Obadiah, a meeting was brokered that brought King Ahab and Prophet Elijah face to face. During this meeting, at which Ahab accused Elijah as the "Troubler of Israel", Elijah proposed a contest between himself, as ambassador of the Sovereign God, and the prophets of Baal representing the king of Israel.

Instead of worshiping the Sovereign God, King Ahab and his

wife Jezebel had led God's chosen people to follow the ways of Baal, the Canaanite god. They had convinced the people of Israel that this heathen deity had the ability to provide his adherents with the strength to enjoy all manner of sexual pleasure.

The people liked Baal worship because it accommodated their immoral sexual delights. Temple sex and child sacrifice were rampant in that society. These were practices which God's laws did not permit. But Baal worship gave these godless Kings and the people the freedom to engage in these sins. So, they served Baal and Asherah.

On the day of the contest, King Ahab invited the four hundred prophets of Baal and the four hundred and fifty prophets of Asherah to Mount Carmel. And all the children of Israel also gathered there to watch the magical display by these custodians of occult power.

In this contest of magic against miracles, the rules were set. Each group was provided with a bullock to dress and lay it on wood with no fire under it. They were to call on the names of their respective deities, and the one that answered by fire was to be acclaimed as the true God.

The prophets of Baal were the first to dress their bullock. And they laid it on their altar. And from morning to mid-day, they cried out loud to him, prophesying and cutting themselves with knives as was their manner. But there was no answer. This continued to the time of the evening offering, with no result.

But when it was Elijah's turn, he repaired the altar of the Sovereign God that had been abandoned in Israel. Then he took twelve stones, each representing a tribe of the sons of Jacob. And with these stones he built an altar in the name of the Lord and made a trench around the altar.

He then put the wood in order, dressed the bullock accordingly, and laid it on the wood. Thereafter, he asked the people to pour four barrels of water on the offering he had laid on the wood. He asked them to do this a second and a third time.

Then at the time of the offering of the evening sacrifice, Elijah prayed to the Lord God of Abraham, Isaac, and Israel. And as he did, the fire of God came from heaven and consumed the sacrifice, the wood, the stones, and the dust. It even licked up the water that was in the trench (1 kings 18:38).

And when all the people saw this wonder of God, they all fell on their faces and glorified God. Prophet Elijah had single-handedly won the heart of the whole nation back to God. Through his stubborn faith, he had shown that God, and not Baal, was the Supreme, Sovereign, and Almighty God in-charge of all things.

So, all the people worshiped God declaring that, "The Lord, he is God; the Lord, he is God." Then Elijah commanded that they let none of the prophets of Baal escape. They were all arrested and brought down to the brook Kishon. And there, they killed all of them.

When this kind of fire dwells within a natural man that is willing to serve God's purpose, God uses him to do exploits for his kingdom. In the case of prophet Elijah, this fire flowed freely. And it worked mightily in him, and through him, to bring glory to God's name on earth and to his kingdom of heaven.

After the death of King Ahab, Elijah's fiery prophetic ministry became even more dramatic. Ahaziah the King had fallen through a lattice that was in his upper chamber in Samaria. Uncertain about his condition, he sent messengers to inquire of Beelzebub, an idol, whether he would survive.

Beelzebub must not be confused with the Canaanite god Baal that Ahab and Jezebel worshiped. This was a different deity whose temple was in the city of Ekron. He was believed to possess the power of discernment. So, King Ahaz of Israel sought for his services.

However, the matter was revealed to Prophet Elijah by the angel of the Lord who intercepted the King's messengers on their way. King Ahaziah's action was a reproach to the God of Israel. And in stern rebuke for this disrespect, the prophet Elijah ordered the King's messengers back to him with a grim message.

When the King got the news about his death, he was perplexed.

And after he realized that it came from Prophet Elijah, he became angry and sent out soldiers to arrest him. Sadly, the first and second batches of soldiers who went on this mission were consumed by fire from heaven on the instruction of Elijah.

The third captain of fifty soldiers operated differently. He showed respect to the prophet of God and humbly pleaded for his life and for the lives of his soldiers. So, Elijah spared them and followed them to the Palace where he personally delivered the judgment of death on King Ahaz for despising the God of Israel.

> *"And he sent again a captain of the third fifty with his fifty. And the third captain of fifty went up, and came and fell on his knees before Elijah, and besought him, and said unto him, O man of God, I pray thee, let my life, and the life of these fifty thy servants, be precious in thy sight. Behold, there came fire down from heaven, and burnt up the two captains of the former fifties with their fifties: therefore, let my life now be precious in thy sight. And the angel of the Lord said unto Elijah, Go down with him: be not afraid of him. And he arose and went down with him unto the king. And he said unto him, Thus saith the Lord, Forasmuch as thou hast sent messengers to enquire of Beelzebub the god of Ekron, is it not because there is no God in Israel to enquire of his word?*
>
> *Therefore, thou shalt not come down off that bed on which thou art gone up, but shalt surely die."*
> *(2 Kings 1: 13-16)*

Prophet Elijah was a natural man that lived a supernatural life. The fire of God incubated him so much that his personal enemies and haters of God feared him. Whenever he spoke, heaven listened attentively. And when he gave instructions, the earth and all the elements cooperated with his word.

Yet, while he was associated with many uncommon supernatural deeds, he exhibited emotional human traits in his later years that showed him to be human after all. For despite subduing eight hundred and fifty false prophets that served King Ahab and his wife, he fled for his life following a mere threat from Jezebel.

He was in despair during that period and exhibited signs of anguish and misery. While he was not physically ill, he exhibited signs of severe ministerial depression and persistent fear. The man who once ruled over demons and the elements now succumbed to the natural pressures of life.

Although prophet Micaiah was Elijah's contemporary and Elisha was his successor, this great Man of God was a character who for the most part of his life and ministry, worked alone. This made him feel lonely, isolated, and abandoned, for which he prayed that God should end his life.

Despite these human weaknesses, God still acknowledged him as one of his greatest generals on earth. For this reason, God never let him die in the likeness of natural, mortal men. So, when his ministry was over, God gave Elijah the singular honor of riding back to heaven, alive, in "chariots of fire".

God wants all his children to flow in this fire. Because it endows them with the supernatural power to heal the sick, deliver the bound, break evil yokes, terminate curses, covenants, and to cast out demons. There is secret power in this fire to walk in the gift of faith, work miracles, and do exploits for God's kingdom.

PRAYER POINT

1) Evil walls making progress impossible in my life, collapse, in Jesus' name.

2) Hand of fire, oppress all my oppressors, in Jesus' name.

3) Fire of God, pass through my foundation and destroy the wickedness hiding there, in Jesus' name.

4) O Lord, baptize me with fresh fire for ministry, in Jesus' name.

5) Holy Spirit, enable me to know what Jesus really means to me, in Jesus' name.

6) O God, barricade my life with your hedge of Holy Ghost fire, in Jesus' name.

7) Afflictions labeled with my name, catch fire, in Jesus' name.

8) Satanic ants destroying the fruitful seeds in my life, be roasted by fire, in Jesus' name.

9) Fire of God, destroy the locusts attacking my harvest, in Jesus' name.

10) Holy Ghost fire, fill my mouth with songs of deliverance, in Jesus' name.

11) O God, make my heart burn with your fiery touch, in Jesus' name.

12) Holy Spirit, help me proclaim God's greatness with the fire of humble adoration, in Jesus' name.

13) As the Lord lives, the fire of God in my life shall not go out, in Jesus' name.

14) Holy Spirit, help me experience the fire of God's love in ways that far exceed my wildest dreams, in Jesus' name.

CHAPTER 10

THE GOD THAT
ANSWERS BY FIRE

God created all things for the service of humanity. This includes the element known as fire. And even when people try to misuse fire, the good news is that this element, in all its forms, is answerable to the Sovereign God. The Almighty God has absolute authority over all fires, whether spiritual or natural.

In God's dwelling place in heaven, his throne is surrounded by blazing fire. This fire burns ceaselessly, yet it cannot harm God, consume the angels, or scald any of the heavenly hosts. This is a great mystery that is beyond all human understanding.

Everything concerning God is a mystery. And except the things he revealed to man, his presence, his nature, and likeness, are all mysteries which no one can fully comprehend. As a result, no one can really explain them. All these things make God who he is, "The I AM, THAT I AM".

Thus, the nature of the almighty God can only be perceived through his expressed virtues, some of which include his grace, his love, his peace, his mercy, righteousness, and joy in the Holy Ghost. All these attributes are like garlands. They decorate God's personality and adorn his shekinah glory.

This shekinah glory is a symbol of God's divine presence. A

vision of its nature reveals the magnificent beauty, exceptional peace, and flawless holiness of heaven. These foreshadow God's idea of what a perfect world should look like. A kingdom surrounded by holy fire that does not destroy its righteous subjects.

God's fire proceeds from his throne in heaven. It puts a mark of identity and power on God's children. Without that mark, a believer is powerless, helpless, and useless to God, and to his kingdom. Such a Christian will be no more useful in God's kingdom than an unbeliever is to God.

That is why the Devil will do everything he can to stop the manifestation of this fire in a person's life. He could even use very close friends or relatives like he did in the life of Joseph, just to ensure that they put out the gift of the holy fire in a person's life.

"Come now therefore, and let us slay him, and cast him into some pit, and we will say, Some evil beast hath devoured him: and we shall see what will become of his dreams" (Genesis 37: 20).

Life is not about big or small dreams. But it is about the passion to make any dream come to life. Joseph was a young boy who had dreams. And a holy fire also burned in him to see them come to life. His brothers realized this about his life and yielded themselves to the Devil in the attempt to quench his fire.

His ten brothers initially toyed with the idea of killing him. But they later settled with the lesser evil of selling him, for twenty pieces of silver, to Ishmaelite traders. Joseph's dream was God-ordained to save lives. And God anointed him with the fire to keep his dream alive. So, the enemy attacked him.

Lack of fire will keep a child of God in darkness and total bondage. Gideon was in this situation. It kept him in bondage. And for many years he kept hiding from people that should hide from him. But when God kindled the holy fire in his life, he came alive and became desperate for divine assignments.

The devil can give a believer whatever he wants if he can make that person compromise his purpose and not let this holy fire burn in his life. A person will live his life in fear if he does not respond to the voice of God. That way, the enemy will keep him in spiritual prison like he did to Gideon.

The enemy roars like a lion which he is not. But God's voice roars like many waters. So, there is a difference when God speaks to his chosen child. That is when problems melt like wax and darkness disappears without delay because the voice of God is accompanied by intense fire and bright shining light (Psalm 119:105; 18: 13; 46:6)

Every element on earth has its replica existing in heaven. There is an altar in God's tabernacle in heaven which burns with ceaseless fire. It was from this altar that a seraph took a burning coal to cleanse Isaiah's lips and his tongue before he was commissioned for his true ministry.

> *"Then said I, Woe is me! for I am undone; because I am a man of unclean lips, and I dwell in the midst of a people of unclean lips: for mine eyes have seen the King, the LORD of hosts. Then flew one of the seraphims unto me, having a live coal in his hand, which he had taken with the tongs from off the altar: ⁷And he laid it upon my mouth, and said, Lo, this hath touched thy lips; and thine iniquity is taken away, and thy sin purged." (Isaiah 6: 5-7).*

When fire is seen in the dream, it can represent many things. It can be a sign of God's impending wrath or a representation of some imminent trouble. On the other hand, it may also represent healing, deliverance, or call to ministry, if one has been praying for any of these.

Thus, fire can serve some good or evil purposes. But no matter the source of its appearance, the problem it was programmed to accomplish, its consequences, implications, or meaning, the power and the effects of any fire are always under the control of God.

"But now thus saith the LORD that created thee, O Jacob, and he that formed thee, O Israel, Fear not: for I have redeemed thee, I have called thee by thy name; thou art mine. When thou passest through the waters, I will be with thee; and through the rivers, they shall not overflow thee: when thou walkest through the fire, thou shalt not be burned; neither shall the flame kindle upon thee" (Isaiah 43: 1-2).

The phrase, "God that answers by fire", is a figure of speech that describes the blazing speed with which God responds to the prayers of his children. Whenever God's Children, who know their right in Christ call on God, he never delays in answering them.

In the showdown against the combined prophets of Baal and Asherah on Mount Carmel, prophet Elijah cried to God, and he answered expressly. He put an emergency request to heaven and God responded expressly. He wasted no time in sending fire from heaven to consume Elijah's offering. (1 Kings 18: 36-39).

And in the matter of King Ahaziah of Israel who sent batches of soldiers to arrest the man of God; the same prophet Elijah sought for the intervention of fire from heaven, and it came without delay. The fire of God came down as quickly as the prophet of God demanded for it.

The response from heaven was so instant that the soldiers sent by King Ahaziah to arrest prophet Elijah were destroyed before they had the time to react or retreat. This was not a fluke incident, because when a second batch of fifty soldiers and their captain arrived, as backup, the prophet called for another fire.

The fire of God is a gift and a weapon which Christians who understand its power can exploit. It is difficult to hurt anyone under the spiritual cover of this fire. This divine weapon from God's armory makes children literally untouchable and renders their bodies too hot for the enemy to handle.

Holy Fire is a spiritual asset for any all children of God. Prophet Elisha knew that his God answer's by fire. And he always exploited that asset. So, once when his servant noticed that they were surrounded by Syrian soldiers, he was terribly afraid.

But after he reported the matter to his master, he comforted him before taking the issue to the court of heaven. And all prophet Elisha did was just pray a simple prayer. He asked God to open the eyes of this his servant to see that there were more soldiers with them than were with their enemies.

> *"And Elisha prayed, and said, LORD, I pray thee, open his eyes, that he may see. And the LORD opened the eyes of the young man; and he saw: and, behold, the mountain was full of horses and chariots of fire round about Elisha"* *(2 Kings 6: 17).*

Instantly, God opened the eyes of this un-named servant of Elisha. And what he saw overwhelmed him. The mountain-home where he and his master lodged was surrounded by horses and chariots of fire from heaven. Apparently, God sent his chariots of fire ahead to safeguard Elisha and this his servant.

When God is delighted in a person, he baptizes him beyond measures with his fire. He first purges the individuals concerned by removing all the things that hinder God's move in their souls, thereby enabling them to operate in supernatural dimensions for God on earth.

Before God gave the ten commandments to Moses, he spoke to him and all the children of Israel by the foot of Mount Sinai. Prior to this meeting, God insisted that the children of Israel prepare themselves both physically and spiritually for the encounter. Thereafter, God descended upon the mount in thick smoke and fire.

> *"And it came to pass on the third day in the morning, that there were thunders and lightnings, and a thick cloud upon the mount, and the voice of the trumpet exceeding loud; so that all the people that was in the camp trembled. And Moses brought forth the people out of the camp to meet with God; and they stood at the nether part of the mount. And mount Sinai was altogether on a smoke because the LORD descended upon it in fire: and the smoke thereof ascended as the smoke of a furnace, and the whole mount quaked greatly"* (Exodus 19: 16-18).

> *"And ye came near and stood under the mountain; and the mountain burned with fire unto the midst of heaven, with darkness, clouds, and thick darkness. And the LORD spake unto you out of the midst of the fire: ye heard the voice of the words but saw no similitude; only ye heard a voice"* (Deuteronomy 4: 11--12).

God has deposited gifts in every life that are groaning to manifest. But no one will attain his human potential until he is ready to communicate with God in the language of fire. The language of fire enables a person of ordinary human nature to do extraordinary things to the glory of God.

Those who are baptized with fire understand this language and when they speak, heaven answers them by fire. This is how the natural man can accomplish supernatural deeds. In the Bible, there were many ordinary people that God used this way.

> *"For ye see your calling, brethren, how that not many wise men after the flesh, not many mighty, not many noble, are called: But God hath chosen the foolish things of the world to confound the wise; and God hath chosen the weak things of the world to confound the things which are mighty; And base things of the world, and things which are despised, hath God chosen, yea, and things which are not, to bring to nought things that are: That no flesh should glory in his presence"* (1 Corinthians 1: 26--29).

The story of Peter and John in the Book of Acts of the Apostles is one such illustration. The miraculous healing of a thirty-eight-year-old man crippled at birth, who always sat at the Beautiful Gate of the temple begging alms, one day drew public attention. Why? Because two ordinary men did an extraordinary thing.

Everyone, including the high priest and other Jewish religious leaders were astonished at this astounding miracle. Rightly, they conceded that it was done by men who were unlearned in the law of Moses. But the multitude took note that these men were with Jesus, which explained the source of their power.

No Christian can make any ministerial progress in his work for "the God that answers by fire" without the anointing of fire sitting on his life. When a person is incubated by this fire, no fire of the enemy cannot consume him. And the measure of that fire in any life determines how much God can use him to do.

That explains why Bible characters like Moses, Samuel, Daniel, and apostle Paul, just to name a few, excelled greatly in their respective ministries. They knew the God they served, trusted him, and he used them to enthrone and dethrone kings, bind the mouth of lions, and to raise the dead.

A person that is filled with the fire of God will readily receive answers from "the God that answers by fire". He makes them ready to take the battle to the camp of their enemies instead of being on the receiving end all the time. When God answers a Christian by fire, he quenches the fires that make that life unbearable.

> *"My brethren, count it all joy when ye fall into divers temptations; Knowing this, that the trying of your faith worketh patience. But let patience have her perfect work, that ye may be perfect and entire, wanting nothing" (James 1:2-4).*

God knows whenever a Christian is passing through any challenge. He is aware, whether it is an affliction by the devil, or is part of God's design to prepare that soul ready for a higher-ground assignment. So, keeping a good attitude while in prayer will help to attract the attention of "the God that answers by fire".

The God that answers by fire is himself a consuming fire. Those who know him for his faithfulness can trust to defeat any problem before them if they invite him into their battle. That was how David defeated Goliath and was able to pursue, overtake, and recover all, from Amalekite bandits that raided his camp.

The God that answers by fire used Elijah mightily to show that he, God, and not Baal, is the one that gives rain across the earth and causes the dew to descend from the night skies to irrigate the land. God, no doubt, is the creator of rain and dew. And he proved this matter before all doubters, through prophet Elijah.

The fire power of God in Elijah's life was legendary. It burned so brazenly, and God's light shined so brightly in his life that kings and queens feared him. And even now in this generation, men still glorify the God of heaven and earth when they pray, by calling on the God of Elijah.

> *"And Elijah answered and said to the captain of fifty, If I be a man of God, then let fire come down from heaven, and consume thee and thy*

fifty. And there came down fire from heaven and consumed him and his fifty. Again, also he sent unto him another captain of fifty with his fifty. And he answered and said unto him, O man of God, thus hath the king said, Come down quickly. And Elijah answered and said unto them, If I be a man of God, let fire come down from heaven, and consume thee and thy fifty. And the fire of God came down from heaven and consumed him and his fifty" (2 Kings 1: 10--12).

The enemy will trample upon anyone who fails to exploit his privilege as a child of the God that answers by fire. That person will end up in his adversary's furnace of affliction. He may not totally destroy that Christian, but will make it difficult for that individual to recover control of himself.

But the child of God that is "hot on fire" will not be burned by his enemy's fire. When a child of God understands that he serves "the God that answers by fire", he will lean on the name of his God. This has enabled many people of faith to outwit the devil's agenda like Hananiah, Mishael, and Azariah did.

"But now thus saith the LORD that created thee, O Jacob, and he that formed thee, O Israel, Fear not: for I have redeemed thee, I have called thee by thy name; thou art mine. When thou passest through the waters, I will be with thee; and through the rivers, they shall not overflow thee: when thou walkest through the fire, thou shalt not be burned; neither shall the flame kindle upon thee." (Isaiah 43: 1-2).

Despite the Adamic nature of sin through which all men are born, God promises to protect everyone redeemed by the blood of

Jesus from spiritual and physical afflictions. He is faithful to all who trust that he can answer by fire, and he does not forsake them in the time of their affliction.

God's fire is a weapon of deliverance for believers who find themselves in the wicked flames of life. He comes quickly to those who call on him and as a shield of protection he preserves their souls, in times of misery, until they are established in a place of safety. (Psalm 18:11-14; 66:12).

Oftentimes, people wonder how some Christians go through tough trials when others are unable to bear the slightest pain in life. They do not understand how God fights for some people while others are left to cope on their own even after they have fasted and prayed to the same God.

The difference is staying close to "the God that answers by fire". When you stay under the cover of his fire, you become a member of the inner caucus. When there is a campfire, it is usually the people in the ring closest to the fire that feel the warmest.

Firebrand Christians are those closest to God. Their human spirits are joined to God's Holy Spirit through Christ in ceaseless prayers and thanksgiving. As a result, they can handle any situation, while remaining joyful in hope, patient in affliction, and faithful in prayer.

God gave mankind the tremendous privilege to engage in a relationship with him. But it is the respective responsibilities of all lovers of God to fight to keep this relationship in great shape. This is because the enemy understands the benefits of it to mankind and has therefore decided to bring it under serious attack.

The Devil knows that he cannot possess any person's soul if that individual is loyal to God and is very dedicated in his relationship and fellowship with his maker. That is why he fights believers, attacking their faith and everything they stand to gain from God.

Every relationship is designed to add value to someone's life or take away something precious from him. But while the relationship with God improves human life, any friendship with the Devil devalues the life of the unfortunate victims he arrests.

Everyone that is in a relationship with Christ has a clear chance of receiving the gifts to save, heal, and deliver souls in his society. But friends of Satan can only boast of the tragedies, pain, and sorrow the enemy uses them to inflict on the entire humanity.

The valuable relationship that God desires is exactly what the devil does not want to exist between God and anyone. He understands that friendship with God is the key to empowered Christian life. And that is why the Devil restlessly attacks every believer's relationship with Christ.

The power of the God that answers by fire sets believers apart in times of inevitable affliction. And it distinguishes the Christian whose spirit is filled with the character of Jesus from the one whose head is only filled with Bible scriptures. That explains why faithful Holy Ghost fire-filled Christians are unstoppable.

In the face of most difficult challenges, Christians of this caliber express joy and are thankful. This is not to downplay their genuine pain or suffering, but only because they trust that their redemption by the Holy Spirit, the helper, the evil yoke breaker and evil burden remover, is very nearby.

The God that answers by fire is always close to the faithful. He is there to sustain the believer's hope even in hopeless situations. A child of God animated by the God that answers by fire will handle any challenge, come out as a shining image of Christ, and be ready to move mountains to the glory of God.

Such Christians are never scared of roaring lions, raging floods, or menacing enemies, because they know the source of their strength. When God that answers by fire is by your side, prison doors open on their own accord, chains are broken, and captives are set free, just with simple prayers.

Every Christian is a friend of God through Christ. And as potential friends of the God that answers by fire, they must aspire to speak with boldness and with fire. Heaven is always on red alert waiting for instructions from them. It is the cry of such faithful children of God that provokes the release of the chariots of fire.

The language of fire is powerful. This spiritual language will position the natural man who understands it to be in perfect alignment with the communication pattern in heaven. And anyone who is so connected to it will have the ability to know the mind of God and readily do his will.

Such Holy Ghost filled, fire-baptized believers will also have the ability to give instructions to heaven and instantly get results that enable them control things on earth. This lifestyle comes with developing intimacy with the Holy Spirit just as Jesus had with the Father (John 14:12).

God spoke to men like Abraham and Moses regularly and they clearly heard from him. But in the current dispensation of the divine Holy Spirit, Christians are now even in a better spiritual state than these ancient Characters to communicate with God.

Christians no longer have to go to the tabernacle, like Moses often did to hear from God. They are now with God wherever they are, because by the Spirit of adoption, all believers have been brought into an intimate relationship with God where they can have honest conversations with him as the Abba Father (Romans 8:15–17,26–27).

When a soul surrenders to the God that answers by fire, that life begins to reign with Christ. Defeat starts to give way to victory, and failure becomes history. Uncommon and out-of-season great things become routine in that life or through it, that could not happen ordinarily before.

Indeed, "the God that answers by fire" is the Sovereign God. He is also the God that speaks with thunder coming from his mouth. He is the God who does wonders, whose voice is like the sound of many waters. From under the cover of his thunderous voice, he readily answers his children and rescues them.

When he speaks, flashes of lightning as the pearls of thunder bellow from his tabernacle that is in heaven where seven lamps of never-ceasing fire burn. And whenever this God stretches forth his staff in the sky, thunder and hail run down to the earth.

It is from there, that "the God that answers by fire" silences those who contend with him. It is from this fiery throne that he brings judgment upon the ends of the earth, gives strength to the faithful, exalts the horn of his anointed, gives power to the faint, and increases strength to those that have no might.

> *"He giveth power to the faint; and to them that have no might he increaseth strength. Even the youths shall faint and be weary, and the young men shall utterly fall: But they that wait upon the LORD shall renew their strength; they shall mount up with wings as eagles; they shall run, and not be weary; and they shall walk, and not faint" (Isaiah 40: 29-31).*

> *"I will call upon the LORD, who is worthy to be praised: so shall I be saved from mine enemies"* (Psalm 18: 3)

The greatest need of every Christian should be the desire to be in fellowship with "this God that answers by Fire". In a dark world ravaged by betrayal, distrust, disease and sickness, poverty, hardships, and racial hatred, all the world needs today is friendship and fellowship with "the God that answers by fire".

Because many have succumbed to materialism and godlessness has become the deadliest disease, every soul needs this God. As the creator of the universe, he is the only one who can save it. He saved mankind before on the cross and he is coming again for those whose relationship with Jesus is alive.

PRAYER POINTS.

1) Fire of God in my bones, connect me to the throne of grace, in Jesus' name.

2) Fire of God, warm up my heart to help the helpless, in Jesus' name.

3) Fire of revival pass through this land and set it ablaze afresh, in Jesus' name.

4) Hand of fire, lift me from the valley of defeat to the mountain of victory, in Jesus' name.

5) Evil obstacles holding me stagnant be melted by fire, in Jesus' name.

6) Holy Spirit, breathe your fresh fire upon my soul, in Jesus' name.

7) Fire of God, burn in every environment where I am present, in Jesus' name.

8) Holy Spirit, back God's word in my mouth, with your fire, in Jesus' name.

9) Holy Fire, purge every filthiness in my life, in Jesus' name.

10) Holy Spirit, connect my prayers to the will of God, in Jesus' name.

11) God of signs and wonders, show yourself in my situation, in Jesus' name.

12) Wall of Holy Ghost fire, protect all my organs, in Jesus' name.

13) God's angel with sword of fire, protect the garden of my life, in Jesus' name.

14) Angel with feet like fire, go before me, walk behind, and around me, in Jesus' name.

Printed in the United States
by Baker & Taylor Publisher Services